Perfecting Leadership in Private Equity

Lead beyond the Deal

A revised 1st Edition

Mohamad Chahine

MeritIP Publishing

Copyright

Copyright © 2024 by Mohamad Chahine. All rights reserved.

No part of this book may be reproduced, stored in a retrieval system, or transmitted in any form or by any means—electronic, mechanical, photocopying, recording, or otherwise—without prior written permission from the publisher or author, except as permitted by U.S. copyright law.

"The most important thing about an investment is the kind of person that is running it."

Warren Buffet

Author's Quote

"In Private Equity, you will only lead well when you learn to lead beyond the deal. For beyond the deal and the dough lie the true riches—being true to your values, fair in your actions, and kind to those around you.

Inspiration is boomerang kindness.

Be genuine—**soft as a rose, yet firm as its thorns.**

Let them love you, fear you, and respect you all at once.

Trade with the bees and the worms, and always **rise through all seasons."**

...And when the worms come to **claim their debt,** dealstones fade as if never made, and your tombstone longs to read:

"A dear friend, a loving parent, a spouse to someone that eventually matters."

Table of Contents

Copyright	3
Dedication	11
Introduction	12
Why I Wrote the Book	15
Section 1: A Leadership Primer	17
What is Leadership?	18
The Anti-Leader	21
Leadership Qualities: Primary and Secondary	25
Leadership: Walking and Talking the Unbeaten Path	30
Substances that Shine: The Glitter and The Gold	35
The Spectrum of Leadership: Beyond Extroversion and Introversion	38
The Darwin Prize of Epic Fails	41
Leading to Failure: Lessons Never Learnt	44
The Chronicles of Leadership Lessons	44
Leadership: Eternal or with an Expiry Date?	47
Prospecting and Introspecting: Are Leaders Born or Made?	50
Unveiling Leadership: Beyond Binary Constructs	50
Leadership Styles: Navigating the Weather Patterns	53
Leadership: A Personal and Circumstantial Affair	57

Leaders and Leader Makers: The Hidden Architects   60
    Unveiling the Architects of Leadership   60

Leadership Turfs: The Overcrowded Leaderscape   63
    The Coalescence of Leadership: A Synergetic or Chaotic Fusion?   64

The Strategic Pause: The Unseen Power in Leadership   67

Harnessing Leadership Spikes: The Essence of Transformational Influence   70

The Paragon of Leadership: In Search of the Uber Leader   73

Navigating the Economy of Leadership: Investments and Returns   76
    The Economics of Leadership: A Four-Dimensional Analysis   76

Section 2: A Crash Course - Private Equity 101   80

Part 1: Private Equity - The Industry   81

Understanding Private Equity   85

The Private Equity Process   87

Private Equity Fund Structure   89

Access to Private Equity   92

PE Lifecycle and Mechanisms   94

Valuation in Private Equity   97

Fees and the J-Curve   100

Risks in Private Equity   103

New Trends in Private Equity   106

Global Private Equity AUM: A Titan's Grasp on Global Business   109

Demystifying Private Equity: Beyond the Acronym	112
Part 2: Private Equity - The Players	114
The PE Players: Deal Teams and Operational Value Creation Teams	115
Part 2a: The Players – The PE Deal Teams	117
The Role of Deal Teams in PE	118
Anatomy of a PE Deal	121
Deal Sourcing and Evaluation Strategies	125
Deal Execution and Portfolio Integration	128
Portfolio Management and Value Maximization	132
The Evolving Role of Deal Teams in PE	135
Part 2b: The Players - OVC and Operational Partners	138
The Essence of Operational Value Creation in PE	139
Operational Partners: The Architects of Value	142
OVC Strategies and Implementation	145
Measuring the Impact of OVC and OP Engagement	148
The BHAG Approach	151
The Future of OVC and OP in Private Equity	153
Deal Teams and Operating Partners: Compare and Contrast	156
Section 3: Leadership Excellence in Private Equity	159
Understanding leadership in Private Equity	160
The Role of the PE Leader	165

Building and Leading High-Performing Deal Teams	168
Adaptive Leadership as a Strategy in Private Equity	172
Navigating People Challenges and Risks in PE Leadership	175
Streamlining Steadfast Leadership during Crisis, Challenge and Change	178
To Lead in PE is to be the Mantra, Mentor and Mentee	182
The 7-Step Roadmap to Mastering PE-Wisdom Leadership	184
Case Studies on Impactful and Adaptive PE Leadership	**189**
Case Study 1: The Rise of Vista Equity Partners – How Robert Smith Revolutionized Software Private Equity	*189*
Case Study 2: Warburg Pincus and the Transformation of Avalara – Scaling a Tax Technology Leader	*192*
Case Study 3: How EQT Transformed SUSE into a European Tech Powerhouse	*194*
Appendix	**197**
Case Studies of Inspirational and Exceptional PE Leadership	**203**
Case 1: Henry Kravis & George Roberts – Pioneering the Leveraged Buyout	*203*
Case 2: Robert Smith – Building a Tech-Focused PE Empire	*205*
Case 3: Orlando Bravo – The "Godfather of Software Private Equity"	*207*
PE Leadership Trivia: Did You Know?	*209*
Afterword	**213**
About the Author	**215**

Dedication

To the leaders who shape the future—not through titles or authority, but through vision, resilience, and the courage to navigate uncertainty.

This book is dedicated to those who lead not by demanding loyalty, but by inspiring trust—the professionals, mentors, and decision-makers in private equity who understand that leadership is not about control, but about **empowering others, driving transformation, and making decisions that stand the test of time.**

True leadership is not measured in headlines or accolades but in the silent moments of difficult choices, unwavering commitment, and the ability to guide teams through complexity and change. It is found in those who **listen before they act, learn before they teach, and serve before they command.**

May this book be both a **compass and a catalyst**—guiding those who strive not just for power, but for **lasting impact**. Because leadership is not about standing above others, but about **lifting those around you to greater heights.**

*...And to my **lovely wife and children**, who have endured the long nights, endless travel, and the many deals I once obsessed over—only for them to be **long forgotten, sold, and written off**. Yet, while those deals are gone, **your love remains**, and there's nothing I appreciate more than seeing you spend the money I earned from them!!! **No one deserves it more than you.** Enjoy it—just don't ask me to do it all over again.*

Introduction

In the uncharted waters of the global economy and with break Leadership in Private Equity (PE) is distinct from leadership in other industries. It is high-pressure, fast-moving, and deeply tied to the success of businesses that investors expect to scale, restructure, or exit within a limited timeframe. The ability to lead effectively in this environment is not just about making strategic decisions—it's about execution, alignment, and adaptability.

With **25 years of experience** across the full PE cycle—as a **Deal Team member, Operating Partner, Interim CEO, and Fractional CEO**—I have seen what works and what does not. Leadership in PE is not just about leading a company; it is about leading across companies, across industries, and often under time constraints that demand results.

I chose not to write this book as a personal account. PE leadership is too broad for one person's experience to be the defining perspective. Instead, this is a **reference guide**—a structured collection of **tested leadership principles** that have been applied in real investment environments. These insights are drawn from the realities of PE, where leadership is not about theory, but about **outcomes**.

How This Book is Structured

This book is divided into three sections, each covering a different aspect of PE leadership:

1. The Leadership Compass

This section defines what makes a strong leader in PE. It covers:

- The essential qualities of PE leadership, including **strategic thinking, execution, and resilience**.
- The **common pitfalls** that leaders face in high-stakes environments.
- The difference between leadership in PE and leadership in traditional corporate settings.

2. The Private Equity Map

This section provides an overview of PE from a leadership perspective:

- The **structure of PE firms** and leadership responsibilities at different levels.
- The **PE investment process** and the role of leadership at each stage.
- The **challenges of managing portfolio companies**, from acquisition to exit.

3. Leadership Within the PE Landscape

This section connects leadership principles to the realities of PE. It includes:

- **Practical strategies** used by experienced PE leaders.
- **Case studies** that illustrate effective decision-making.

- A **7-Step Roadmap** to help leaders develop and refine their approach.

Who This Book is For

This book is for professionals working in PE who want to strengthen their leadership skills, including:

- **PE Dealmakers and Fund Managers** – Those responsible for sourcing and executing investments.
- **Operating Partners and PE-Backed Executives** – Leaders who drive value creation in portfolio companies.
- **Aspiring Leaders in Private Equity** – Professionals preparing to take on leadership roles.

Whether you are already leading investment teams or preparing for a future leadership role, this book provides **practical strategies** that align with the demands of the industry.

Why Leadership in Private Equity Matters

Strong leadership is a key driver of success in PE. It impacts **deal execution, value creation, and the ability to align investors, management teams, and operating partners toward a common goal**. Unlike corporate leadership, which often operates on long-term cycles, leadership in PE is about achieving **measurable results within strict timeframes**.

This book is not a collection of general leadership advice. It is a **practical resource**, designed to provide **clear, applicable strategies** for leadership in the unique environment of Private Equity.

Why I Wrote the Book

Filling a Leadership Gap in Private Equity

Over the years, I've worked across the full **Private Equity (PE) cycle**—as part of deal teams, in operating partner roles, and as an interim and fractional CEO. Through these experiences, one thing became clear: **there is no structured guide to leadership in PE.**

Many leadership books offer **general principles**, while PE books focus on **technical deal-making**. But leadership in PE is different. It requires a mix of **strategic decision-making, operational execution, and the ability to drive change in high-stakes environments**—all within strict investment timelines.

This book was written to **fill that gap**—to serve as a practical, structured resource for those who need **tested leadership strategies, not just theory.**

A Practical Guide for Those in the Field

I didn't want to write a book filled with abstract leadership theories. Leadership in PE is about **real-world challenges**—aligning investors and management teams, making tough calls in uncertain conditions, and delivering value quickly.

This book is designed for:

- **PE professionals transitioning into leadership roles** who need a clear understanding of what is expected.
- **Dealmakers, operating partners, and PE-backed executives** who want to lead more effectively.

- **Anyone in private equity** who recognizes that leadership is about more than just making deals—it's about **execution, adaptability, and long-term value creation.**

The goal was to make this book **accessible and useful, whether you are new to PE leadership or looking to refine your approach.** It combines practical frameworks, industry insights, and strategies that can be applied immediately.

Leadership in PE Is About Execution, Not Just Strategy

Many leadership books focus on **vision and inspiration**, which are important—but in PE, leadership is also about **execution.**

- How do you lead a newly acquired company with an urgent turnaround mandate?
- How do you drive value creation across multiple portfolio companies?
- How do you manage investor expectations while keeping management teams engaged?

These are the real challenges PE leaders face, and this book is built around **providing direct answers to those questions.**

More Than Just Financial Success

Great PE leadership isn't just about maximizing returns. It's about **building strong teams, making the right strategic decisions, and leading in a way that drives sustainable growth.**

I wrote this book because I believe leadership in PE is **one of the most demanding yet under-discussed aspects of the industry.** My hope is that this resource will provide clarity, challenge traditional thinking, and help shape **better, stronger, and more adaptable PE leaders.**

Section 1: A Leadership Primer

What is Leadership?

"Leadership is about making others better as a result of your presence and making sure that impact lasts in your absence." - Sheryl Sandberg

Leadership is a dynamic and complex phenomenon that encompasses various elements, styles, and approaches. It is about guiding others to achieve a common goal, influencing with integrity, and inspiring change. Understanding the essence of leadership is crucial for anyone aspiring to lead effectively or study the dynamics of leadership within organizations.

The Essence of Leadership: Leadership can be distilled into a set of core elements that characterize effective leadership:

- **Vision**: Crafting and articulating a clear and compelling direction for the future.
- **Integrity**: Acting with honesty, ethics, and moral principles.
- **Communication**: Effectively conveying ideas, information, and goals.
- **Empathy**: Understanding and connecting with the emotions and experiences of others.
- **Influence**: Inspiring and motivating others towards a shared vision.
- **Adaptability**: Navigating change and uncertainty with grace.
- **Courage**: Taking bold actions and facing challenges with resilience.
- **Inspiration**: Igniting passion and commitment in others.

- **Decision-making**: Making timely and effective choices.
- **Resilience**: Bouncing back from setbacks and persevering in the face of adversity.
- **Empowerment**: Enabling others to reach their full potential.
- **Innovation**: Fostering creativity and driving progress.
- **Collaboration**: Promoting teamwork and collective achievement.
- **Humility**: Cultivating openness, self-awareness, and a willingness to learn from others.

Leadership Styles and Approaches: Leadership styles vary based on the leader's behavior and approach to leading others:

- **Authoritative**: Setting clear expectations and making decisions without seeking input from others.
- **Democratic**: Encouraging participation and collaboration among team members.
- **Servant**: Prioritizing the needs of others and focusing on serving the team.
- **Transformational**: Inspiring and motivating followers to achieve higher levels of performance.
- **Transactional**: Emphasizing reward and punishment based on performance.
- **Situational**: Adapting leadership style to match the needs of the situation and the capabilities of followers.

The Role of Context in Leadership: Leadership effectiveness is influenced by various contextual factors, including organizational culture, team dynamics, and external environmental conditions:

- **Organizational culture**: Shapes the norms, values, and behaviors within an organization and influences leadership style and effectiveness.
- **Team dynamics**: Impact how leadership is enacted and experienced within a group.

Leaders must adapt their leadership style to suit the context and effectively address the challenges and opportunities present in their environment.

The Development of Leadership Skills: Leadership skills can be developed and honed over time through experience, education, and deliberate practice. Leadership is primarily a learned behavior that can be enhanced through training and development. Continuous learning, self-reflection, and seeking opportunities for growth are essential for aspiring leaders to enhance their leadership skills and capabilities.

This foundation in understanding the multifaceted nature of leadership without tying it specifically to any one sector allows for a broad application of these principles. It sets the stage for more detailed exploration in subsequent sections, ensuring a comprehensive approach to leadership across various contexts.

The Anti-Leader

"Leadership is not about the title or the position. It's about the impact, influence, and inspiration you provide to others, regardless of your role."
— Robin Sharma

Rethinking Leadership: What It Is Not

Understanding **what leadership is not** can be just as important as defining what it truly is. Too often, leadership is mistaken for **authority, dominance, or personal success**, but in reality, **great leaders create environments where others succeed**. This chapter dismantles common myths, shedding light on what **true leadership looks like**—and what it does not.

Common Leadership Myths & Misconceptions

- **Leadership vs. Dictatorship** – Leadership is about **inspiring and guiding**, not **controlling**. True leaders **foster collaboration and empowerment** rather than demanding obedience.

- **Not a Solo Journey** – Leadership is not about **carrying the burden alone** but about **leveraging the collective strengths of a team** for shared success.

- **Beyond Titles** – Influence and impact **define leadership**, not job titles or hierarchy. Some of the most **effective leaders don't sit at the top—they drive change from anywhere.**

- **Embracing Imperfection** – Effective leaders acknowledge **mistakes and vulnerabilities**, using them as opportunities for learning and growth.

- **Respect Over Popularity** – Leadership isn't about **being liked**; it's about **doing what's right** for the team and the organization, even when the decisions are tough.

- **Empowerment Over Control** – The best leaders **trust and empower** their teams, encouraging autonomy and innovation rather than micromanaging.

- **Serving Others, Not Just Yourself** – Leadership is about **lifting others up**, not advancing personal agendas. True leaders measure success **by the impact they have on those around them**.

The Anti-Leader vs. The Anti-Follower

Not all who hold leadership positions **are true leaders**—some fall into the trap of **being anti-leaders**, undermining trust, stifling creativity, and prioritizing self-interest over team success. Similarly, **anti-followers** resist guidance, reject accountability, and fail to contribute constructively.

The Anti-Leader:
✘ Seeks control rather than collaboration
✘ Takes credit for successes, shifts blame for failures
✘ Leads by fear rather than respect
✘ Avoids difficult conversations and decisions
✘ Prioritizes personal ambition over team well-being

The Anti-Follower:
✘ Resists feedback and refuses to adapt
✘ Complains without offering solutions
✘ Works in isolation instead of collaborating
✘ Follows instructions blindly without critical thinking
✘ Avoids responsibility when things go wrong

Recognizing these behaviors—both in leaders and followers—is key to **creating a culture where people take ownership, work with integrity, and drive real results.**

Case Studies: Tim Cook & Marissa Mayer

Tim Cook – Leading With Influence, Not Ego

When Tim Cook stepped into **Steve Jobs' shoes** as Apple's CEO, many doubted whether he could **match Jobs' legendary leadership style**. But Cook didn't try to **imitate Jobs**—instead, he **leaned into his strengths** as a leader who **listened, empowered others, and led with quiet influence.**

- Focused on **team collaboration and long-term impact** rather than personal visibility.
- **Empowered Apple's culture of innovation** without needing to dominate the spotlight.
- Showed that **steady, thoughtful leadership** can be just as effective as visionary, bold leadership.

Tim Cook's success proved that **great leaders don't have to be loud, charismatic, or authoritative—they need to empower others and make smart, value-driven decisions.**

Marissa Mayer – When Leadership Becomes Overcontrol

Marissa Mayer, former CEO of Yahoo, was once seen as **one of Silicon Valley's rising stars**. However, her leadership style quickly became **a case study in what not to do.**

- Implemented **rigid micromanagement**, forcing employees back into offices even when flexible work was proving successful.
- Made **high-pressure, unilateral decisions** that created friction rather than collaboration.

- Focused on **personal success and image**, rather than building a sustainable leadership team.

Mayer's tenure at Yahoo **demonstrated the dangers of top-down control, rigid decision-making, and failing to build trust with a team.**

Final Thought: Leadership Is Influence, Not Authority

Leadership isn't about **power, perfection, or control**—it's about **impact, influence, and trust**. Whether you hold a title or not, the real question is: **Are you making those around you better?**

True leaders **don't demand respect—they earn it. They don't seek control—they build trust. And they don't lead just for results—they lead for the people who make those results possible.**

Leadership Qualities: Primary and Secondary

"Great leaders are willing to sacrifice their own personal interests for the good of the team." - John Wooden

Exploring the intricate web of leadership qualities, we delve into the attributes that underscore effective leadership. This analysis draws upon the fifteen essential elements previously discussed, highlighting the eight primary qualities identified as foundational by business experts, alongside the seven secondaries, yet equally vital, qualities that enable and support leadership effectiveness.

The Primary Qualities of Leadership

Vision: The North Star of Leadership

Vision acts as the guiding light for organizations and teams, offering a clear path forward. Leaders with vision inspire action and progress, setting the stage for innovation.

Integrity: The Bedrock of Trust

Integrity is crucial in building trust within an organization. Leaders who exemplify honesty and ethical conduct garner respect and loyalty, foundational for ethical leadership.

Communication: The Bridge to Understanding

Effective leaders are adept communicators, capable of sharing ideas and goals in a way that fosters collaboration and alignment towards common objectives.

Empathy: The Heartbeat of Connection

Understanding and connecting with others' experiences and emotions, empathy allows leaders to build deeper relationships and cultivate a supportive and inclusive culture.

Accountability: The Cornerstone of Responsibility

A commitment to accountability ensures leaders and their teams uphold commitments, fostering a culture of integrity and continuous improvement.

Adaptability: The Key to Resilience

The ability to navigate change and uncertainty with resilience is vital. Adaptable leaders can pivot strategies and learn from challenges, guiding their teams through adversity.

Influence: The Power of Persuasion

Influential leaders inspire and motivate, driving collective efforts towards shared achievements and change.

Collaboration: The Symphony of Teamwork

Promoting teamwork and leveraging diverse perspectives, collaboration leads to creativity, innovation, and shared success.

The Secondary Qualities of Leadership

The Secondary Qualities of Leadership - Top 5

1. Courage
The essence of bravery in making tough decisions and facing challenges head-on. Leaders must take calculated risks, stand up for their principles, and protect their team when necessary, including having difficult conversations and admitting mistakes.

2. Inspiration
Motivating teams towards excellence and embodying the organization's values. Great leaders spark enthusiasm through their actions and words, share compelling stories, celebrate successes, and create an environment where people feel energized to give their best.

3. Decision-making
Making sound, timely choices that drive organizational progress. Leaders gather diverse perspectives, analyze data carefully, and balance short-term needs with long-term goals, remaining accountable for outcomes.

4. Adaptability
Demonstrating flexibility and resilience in the face of change. Strong leaders pivot strategies when circumstances shift, help teams navigate uncertainty, and view challenges as opportunities for growth while staying current with industry trends.

5. Innovation
Fostering a culture of creative problem-solving and continuous improvement. Forward-thinking leaders encourage experimentation, create safe spaces for new ideas, and support calculated risk-taking while embracing emerging technologies and methodologies.

Courage: The Essence of Bravery

Leadership demands the courage to make tough decisions and face challenges, inspiring others with fearlessness and ambition.

Inspiration: Igniting Passion

Inspirational leaders motivate their teams towards excellence, embodying the organization's values and vision to spark enthusiasm and dedication.

Decision-making: The Art of Choice

Effective leadership is characterized by sound decision-making, involving thorough analysis and timely, informed choices that drive organizational progress.

Resilience: The Strength to Persevere

Resilient leaders maintain focus and composure through adversity, fostering a culture of determination and confidence among their teams.

Empowerment: Enabling Others

By delegating authority and trusting in their team's capabilities, empowering leaders foster innovation, autonomy, and meaningful contribution.

Innovation: Cultivating Creativity

Innovative leadership encourages new ideas and continuous improvement, creating an environment where creativity thrives and challenges the status quo.

Collaboration: Fostering Team Unity

Emphasizing teamwork and cooperation, collaborative leadership values diverse perspectives and shared goals, enhancing innovation and productivity.

The interplay of these fifteen qualities forms the foundation of effective leadership, each contributing to an integrated approach that drives organizational success. Leaders who embody these attributes can navigate complexities, inspire their teams, and foster growth and innovation.

Alan Mulally at Ford Motor Company

Alan Mulally's tenure at Ford is a testament to the power of **visionary leadership, clear communication, and collaborative problem-solving.** At a time when Ford faced **severe financial distress**, Mulally's strategic vision and leadership approach not only steered the company away from collapse but also repositioned it as **a global leader in innovation and sustainability.**

His success highlights the **transformative impact of leadership that balances both strategic direction and people-centric management.** By fostering **transparency, accountability, and a culture of shared purpose**, Mulally laid the foundation for **long-term resilience and industry leadership.**

His approach serves as a blueprint for leaders across industries—demonstrating that **clear vision, decisive action, and the ability to inspire others** are essential for driving meaningful and lasting success.

Leadership: Walking and Talking the Unbeaten Path

"Great leaders inspire greatness in others."

- Lolly Daskal

Effective leadership demands a delicate balance between action and words, embodying the principles of both "Walking the Talk" and "Talking the Walk." This chapter explores the critical behaviors and communication strategies that distinguish truly impactful leaders, emphasizing the importance of consistency between what leaders say and do. Through this alignment, leaders can inspire, motivate, and guide their teams towards success, navigating the path less traveled with integrity and vision.

The Dos and Don'ts of a Leader

Leadership is characterized not only by actions but also by the avoidance of behaviors that can undermine team spirit and productivity. Here, we delineate the positive actions that build a constructive work environment against the negative behaviors that could stifle growth and collaboration.

Positive Leadership Behaviors:

- Arriving at work on time, exemplifying punctuality, and respect for others' time.
- Completing tasks diligently, highlighting commitment and responsibility.

- Communicating effectively, ensuring transparency, and fostering trust.
- Collaborating with team members, valuing each person's contribution.
- Seeking and embracing feedback for continuous improvement.
- Respecting diverse opinions, cultivating an inclusive workplace.
- Taking responsibility for actions, demonstrating accountability and integrity.

Behaviors to Avoid:

- Procrastination and tardiness, which show disregard for team dynamics.
- Withholding information, creating barriers to trust and collaboration.
- Working in isolation, neglecting the power of collective effort.
- Resisting feedback and refusing to learn, stifling personal and team growth.

The Say and Say Not of a Leader

The language of leadership significantly impacts team morale and effectiveness. Phrases that affirm, encourage, and support can uplift and empower teams, while dismissive or negative comments can erode trust and confidence.

Lead by Example: "Walk the Talk" and "Talk the Walk"

Leadership excellence comes from the congruence of actions and words, especially when charting new courses.

"Walk the Talk" (Actions):

- Demonstrating punctuality and commitment.
- Completing tasks and meeting deadlines, setting a standard for accountability.
- Communicating transparently and fostering an environment of openness.
- Supporting team members actively, showing genuine interest and engagement.

"Talk the Walk" (Communication):

- Expressing confidence in the team, building a foundation of trust.
- Inviting collaboration, valuing diverse insights and ideas.
- Acknowledging contributions, creating a culture of appreciation and respect.

What Leaders Do and Do not

What Leaders Do	What Leaders Do Not Do
Arrive at work on time	Arrive late
Complete assigned tasks	Procrastinate
Communicate effectively with colleagues	Withhold information
Collaborate with team members	Work in isolation
Seek feedback and opportunities for growth	Resist feedback and refuse to learn
Respect others' opinions and perspectives	Disregard others' viewpoints and interrupt conversations
Take responsibility for their actions	Blame others for mistakes
Act with integrity and honesty in all interactions	Engage in deceitful or unethical behavior
Support and assist others when needed	Ignore or dismiss others' needs and concerns
Maintain a positive attitude and outlook	Spread negativity and complain consistently

What Leaders Say and Do not Say

What Leaders Say	What Leaders Never Say
"I believe in you."	"It's not my problem."
"Let's work together to find a solution."	"I don't have time for this."
"Your contributions are valued and appreciated."	"Just do it because I said so."
"I'm here to support you."	"That's not how we've always done it."
"We can learn from this experience and grow stronger."	"I know everything."

Example: Mary Barra, CEO of General Motors

Mary Barra exemplifies the essence of "Walking the Talk" and "Talking the Walk." Her leadership is marked by a hands-on approach and a commitment to transparency, accountability, and collaboration. Barra's interactions with employees across all levels and her clear, consistent communication of GM's values and priorities highlight her dedication to aligning actions with words. This alignment has fostered a culture of trust, empowerment, and excellence at General Motors, highlighting the profound impact of authentic leadership.

By understanding and embodying these principles, leaders can navigate the complexities of their roles with integrity and efficacy, inspiring their teams to achieve greatness and navigate the unbeaten path with confidence and cohesion.

Substances that Shine: The Glitter and The Gold

"True leadership is not about shining brightly; it's about illuminating the path for others."

- Unknown

This section explores the nuanced landscape of leadership, probing beneath the surface of qualities often celebrated in leaders but whose true value may not be as pivotal as commonly perceived. Charisma, humor, technological proficiency, privilege, and unconventional backgrounds—attributes heralded for their allure and potential to differentiate—undergo scrutiny for their actual impact on effective leadership.

Charisma: The Double-Edged Sword

Charisma is frequently lauded as a cornerstone of influential leadership, attributed with the power to draw followers, and inspire action. However, its essence in leadership merits a deeper examination. While charismatic leaders can galvanize teams and foster loyalty, there exists a thin line where charisma may veer into manipulation or become a facade masking substance. Authentic leadership demands more than charm; it requires a foundation built on integrity, vision, and the ability to genuinely connect with others on a meaningful level.

Humor: More Than Just Laughs

Humor serves as a tool to lighten the atmosphere, encourage camaraderie, and bridge communication gaps. Yet, its application within leadership contexts warrants careful consideration.

Misplaced or insensitive humor can alienate individuals, detract from the gravity of leadership responsibilities, and even erode respect. Effective leaders understand the power of humor to unite but also recognize the importance of its judicious use, ensuring it adds value rather than detracts from the leadership ethos.

Technology Savviness: Balancing Digital and Human

In an era where digital capabilities are at the forefront of operational efficiency and innovation, technological savviness is often seen as a crucial leadership trait. Nonetheless, the emphasis on digital proficiency should not overshadow the core of leadership—the human connection. Overreliance on technology risks impairing essential interpersonal skills and creative thinking. Leaders should harness technology as a tool to augment, not replace, the personal interactions and creative processes that drive true leadership success.

Privilege: A Platform, Not a Leadership Credential

Privilege, or "blue blood," often correlates with access to resources and opportunities not widely available. While such advantages can facilitate paths to leadership positions, they do not inherently endow individuals with the qualities necessary for effective leadership. True leadership transcends privilege, focusing on leveraging one's position to enact positive change, empathize with varied perspectives, and champion inclusivity.

Unconventional Backgrounds: Beyond the Narrative

The allure of leaders with unconventional backgrounds—such as those who diverge from traditional educational or career paths—stems from their perceived capacity to bring fresh insights and challenge the status quo. While these attributes can enrich leadership, they are not sole predictors of success. Effective leadership encompasses a blend of experience, perspective, and the ability to navigate complex challenges. Recognizing the value of diverse backgrounds enriches the leadership tapestry but underscores that leadership efficacy is defined by actions and impacts, not just by the path taken.

In distilling the essence of leadership, it becomes evident that the qualities that truly matter extend beyond superficial allure or societal accolades. Effective leadership is rooted in depth of character, a commitment to serve and uplift others, and the pursuit of goals that extend beyond personal gain. It is the leaders who prioritize these foundational principles over the glittering but potentially transient traits who leave a legacy of positive impact and inspired followership.

The Spectrum of Leadership: Beyond Extroversion and Introversion

"Quiet people have the loudest minds."

- Stephen Hawking

The landscape of leadership is often misconstrued as a domain where extroverted traits—outward charisma, assertiveness, and sociability—reign supreme. This perspective overlooks the profound strengths and capabilities that introverted leaders bring to the table. Leadership effectiveness lies not in one's natural inclination toward extroversion or introversion but in leveraging one's inherent qualities to inspire, influence, and innovate.

Embracing the Strengths of Introverted Leadership

Introverted leaders, characterized by their reflective nature and thoughtful approach, offer invaluable insights and leadership styles that complement the dynamism of extroverted leadership. These leaders excel in creating deep connections, fostering an environment of trust, and understanding, and leading through a model of quiet confidence. Their ability to listen attentively and reflect before acting makes them adept at navigating complex challenges and envisioning long-term strategies.

Debunking Myths and Embracing Diversity

- **Myth: Introverted leaders lack effective communication skills.**
  Reality: Introverts often possess profound

communication skills, particularly in one-on-one interactions or written communication, enabling them to articulate their vision and connect deeply with their team members.

- **Myth: Extroverted leaders are inherently more successful.**
  Reality: Success in leadership is not predicated on extroversion. Introverted leaders like Shantanu Narayen of Adobe Inc. have led their companies to new heights through strategic vision, innovation, and fostering a culture of inclusivity and creativity.

- **Myth: Leadership is reserved for 'alpha' personalities.**
  Reality: Effective leadership can manifest in both 'alpha' and 'beta' personality traits, with each bringing unique strengths to leadership roles. The key lies in understanding and leveraging these traits to complement the organizational context and team dynamics.

The Extrovert-Introvert Spectrum in Leadership

The distinction between extroverted and introverted leadership should not be seen as a binary choice but rather as a spectrum, with each leader possessing a unique mix of qualities that can be adapted to various situations. Recognizing and valuing the diversity of leadership styles enables organizations to harness the full potential of their leaders, irrespective of where they fall on the extrovert-introvert spectrum.

A Case Study in Introverted Leadership: Shantanu Narayen of Adobe Inc.

Shantanu Narayen's tenure as CEO exemplifies the power of introverted leadership. His approach—marked by listening, strategic thinking, and empowering others—has propelled Adobe through significant transformations. Under his leadership, Adobe has not only thrived but also set new benchmarks for innovation and growth in the tech industry. Narayen's story is a testament to the fact that leadership is not about how loudly one speaks but about the clarity of one's vision and the ability to guide others toward shared goals.

In conclusion, the essence of effective leadership lies beyond the traditional extrovert-introvert dichotomy. It is about leveraging one's unique strengths, whether they manifest through quiet reflection or dynamic engagement, to inspire greatness in others and lead with purpose and integrity.

The Darwin Prize of Epic Fails

"The greatest teacher, failure is."

- Yoda

In the annals of leadership lore, the "Darwin Prize for Failed Leadership" occupies a unique, albeit dubious, niche. It is a satirical homage to the spectacular misfires in the leadership realm that have unwittingly provided us with invaluable lessons on what not to do. This exploration, drenched in sarcasm, invites us to dissect these failures, not out of mockery, but with a genuine desire to distill wisdom from misjudgment.

The Illustrious Nominees

The Shortsighted Leader: First in line is the leader whose vision was as narrow as a keyhole, propelling their team off the metaphorical cliff with the precision of a misguided missile. This leader, navigating the future with the foresight of a mole, left their team grappling in the dark, a testament to the perils of leadership without foresight.

The Dishonest Leader: Then, we encounter the maestro of mendacity, a leader whose relationship with the truth was as flimsy as a house of cards in a hurricane. They spun tales with the artistry of a seasoned novelist, crafting a world so fantastical it crumbled under the weight of its own fiction, leaving behind a legacy of disillusionment.

The Mute Leader: Silence is golden, or so thought our next nominee, whose communication strategy was akin to a mime performance—enigmatic and utterly baffling. This leader's aversion to articulation turned their leadership into a guessing game, with strategies as decipherable as ancient hieroglyphs sans Rosetta Stone.

The Trustless Leader: Trust, under this leader's reign, became an endangered species, hunted to near extinction. They dismantled trust with the efficiency of a demolition crew, proving that the fastest way to hollow out a team's spirit is through a systematic betrayal of faith.

The Chaos-Inducing Leader: With the organizational acumen of a tornado in a library, this leader turned order into chaos, proving that you can indeed create a storm in a teacup, provided you are oblivious enough to the nuances of leadership.

The Rigid Leader: As flexible as a slab of concrete, this leader's resistance to change was legendary. Anchored in the past, they watched the future pass by like a ship in the night, steadfast in their commitment to yesterday's strategies.

The Innovation-Ignorant Leader: Innovation, in this leader's realm, was as welcome as a skunk at a garden party. They viewed innovative ideas with suspicion, preferring the safety of the known to the risk of novelty, stifling creativity at its source.

The Fearful Leader: Courage fled at the sight of this leader, whose decision-making was as bold as that of a startled rabbit. Paralyzed by fear, they taught us that inaction is indeed an action—of the most perilous kind.

The Accountability-Averse Leader: Dodging responsibility with the agility of a cat, this leader was a virtuoso of evasion. Their mantra? "The buck stops anywhere but here," leaving their team in a perpetual state of bewilderment and frustration.

The Conflict-Catalyst Leader: Harmony's arch-nemesis, this leader had a talent for turning minor disagreements into full-blown feuds, proving that the pen is not mightier than the sword when used to stoke the flames of discord.

The Micromanaging Leader: A leader so ensnared in the minutiae that they lost sight of the horizon. Their overbearing presence smothered initiative, proving that too tight a grip leads to nothing but suffocation.

The Selfish Leader: In their kingdom, "we" was a foreign concept, replaced by the towering "I." Their leadership was a monument to self-interest, leaving a trail of disillusionment in its wake.

The Arrogant Leader: With an ego rivaling that of Narcissus, this leader's self-absorption knew no bounds. They led not with humility but with hubris, alienating those they sought to inspire.

The Exploitative Leader: Viewing their team as mere pawns in their grand scheme, this leader's ambition was as boundless as their empathy was limited. They extracted value with the voracity of a leech, leaving a desolate wasteland of morale in their wake.

Lessons from the Wreckage

As we traverse the hall of infamy, let us not gloat over these tales of leadership gone awry but rather seek the silver linings within these clouds. Each story, each nominee, serves as a beacon, guiding us away from the shoals of failure towards the shores of leadership excellence.

In the shadows of these epic failures lie the luminescence of insight—a guiding light towards becoming the leaders we aspire to be: visionary, honest, communicative, trusting, adaptable, innovative, courageous, accountable, and humble. Let the "Darwin Prize for Failed Leadership" not be a scarlet letter but a catalyst for transformation, urging us to lead with integrity, empathy, and a steadfast commitment to elevating those around us.

Leading to Failure: Lessons Never Learnt

"The only real failure is the failure to try, the unwillingness to take risks." - Sara Blakely

In the tapestry of leadership, the threads of failure weave cautionary tales that resonate through time. The annals of failed leadership—marked by missteps and miscalculations—offer stark landscapes from which aspiring leaders can harvest wisdom. Through the sagas of the **Visionary Vanquished** to the **Humility Forgotten**, we embark on a journey to dissect these narratives, not to dwell on the downfall but to distill the essence of what propels leaders toward unwelcome infamy.

The Chronicles of Leadership Lessons

Visionary Vanquished: The Tale of Blockbuster Video

In an era dominated by digital streams, Blockbuster clung to the relics of rental stores, a testament to the perils of overlooking the digital dawn. Their leadership, veiled in the comfort of past successes, failed to steer the company into the future, marking a cautionary tale of vision lost in the shadows of complacency.

Integrity Incinerated: Volkswagen's Veil

Volkswagen, once a paragon of automotive excellence, found itself ensnared in deception, manipulating truths to mask emissions. This saga of integrity sacrificed on the altar of ambition serves as a stark reminder that the foundation of trust, once shattered, leaves a chasm difficult to bridge.

Communication Catastrophes: United Airlines' Turbulence

A passenger's plight, mishandled and miscommunicated by United Airlines, spiraled into a public relations debacle. The incident underscores the paramount importance of wielding communication not as a tool to deflect but to connect and rectify, lest the brand's image takes flight into the storm.

Trust Tumultuous: Wells Fargo's Woes

In the pursuit of quotas, Wells Fargo veered off the path, creating accounts as phantoms in the night. This breach of trust, a self-inflicted wound, highlights the criticality of upholding the sanctity of customer trust as the cornerstone of organizational integrity.

Organization in Disarray: Healthcare.gov's Hardships

The launch of Healthcare.gov, marred by glitches and gaffes, unveiled a spectacle of disorganization. It serves as a lesson in the quintessential need for meticulous planning and coordination, lest the mission's core becomes obscured by chaos.

Resilience Lacking: Nokia's Nosedive

Once the herald of cellular innovation, Nokia's reluctance to embrace the smartphone revolution exemplifies the dire need for resilience and adaptability. The lesson here is stark; evolve with the tide of innovation or risk being washed away into obscurity.

Innovation Ignored: Kodak's Conundrum

Kodak, the architect of the digital camera, faltered, blinded by the brilliance of its own invention. This narrative of innovation overlooked teaches that the seeds of progress, if not nurtured, can sprout in the gardens of competitors.

Echoes of Lessons Learned

These tales, while draped in the vestiges of failure, illuminate the path forward with beacons of lessons learned. They are not merely stories of what was but guideposts for what could be, urging future leaders to tread with caution, foresight, and an unwavering commitment to the principles that uphold the sanctity of leadership.

As we reflect on these chronicles, let them not be seen as epitaphs on the tombstones of leadership past but as lighthouses guiding us away from the reefs of ruin. For in the heart of failure lies the seeds of wisdom, waiting to be sown by those brave enough to venture into the unknown, armed with the resolve to lead, learn, and leap beyond the echoes of the past.

"**May the Force be with You**" - as we navigate the intricate dance of leadership, may we do so with the grace of those who have learned from the missteps that history so generously shares.

Leadership: Eternal or with an Expiry Date?

In dissecting the essence of leadership, we wade into the debate of its permanence: Is leadership an eternal beacon or does it bear an expiry date, contingent upon the shifting sands of time, results, and perception? This contemplation is not just academic; it is a vital inquiry for anyone vested in the mantle of leadership.

Leadership: A Journey Beyond Time

"In the journey of leadership, success is not measured by the distance covered but by the lives touched, the legacy left, and the enduring impact felt long after the leader has moved on." - Simon Sinek

Leadership, often romanticized as an immutable force, is in reality a tapestry interwoven with the threads of temporal achievements and evolving contexts. The luminosity of a leader's influence, much like the stars in the night sky, can either burn brightly for millennia or fade into obscurity, eclipsed by the advent of new constellations.

The Temporal Tapestry of Leadership

Hindsight's Harvest: Leadership's true measure often lies in the rearview mirror, a posthumous appraisal that either cements its legacy or consigns it to the footnotes of history. The ephemeral nature of leadership is most palpable when once-lauded achievements dim under the shadow of evolving challenges, reminding us that leadership is as much about navigating the present as it is about inscribing oneself into the annals of posterity.

The Sun and the Shadow: The cyclical rise and set of the sun offer a poignant metaphor for leadership's transient essence. Success, the sunlight by which a leader's path is illuminated, demands constant pursuit. The moment inertia sets in, or missteps are made, the shadow of obsolescence begins to loom, challenging leaders to reignite their luminescence or risk fading into the dusk.

Perception's Prism: The longevity of a leader's impact is intricately tied to the prism of perception. The narrative woven around a leader's tenure—crafted through actions, communications, and the alchemy of branding—can either embellish their legacy with an eternal glow or shroud it in the penumbra of forgetfulness. Effective leaders are not just architects of strategy but also of perception, shaping how their leadership is viewed through the kaleidoscope of stakeholder perspectives.

Adaptability or Obsolescence: Leadership's expiry may be triggered not by a depletion of inherent qualities but by a misalignment with the zeitgeist. As the tectonic plates of industry and society shift, so too must leadership adapt, morphing to meet new challenges and expectations. The refusal to evolve, to cling to the relics of past glories, is perhaps the most direct route to obsolescence.

Leadership's Long March: The Case of Howard Schultz

The odyssey of Howard Schultz, Starbucks' architect, epitomizes the undulating journey of leadership. Schultz, hailed for catapulting Starbucks onto the global stage, also navigated turbulent waters—economic recessions, fierce competition, and internal strife. His leadership, once unassailable, faced the crucible of adversity, testing his ability to adapt and rekindle the innovative spirit of Starbucks.

Schultz's resilience and strategic recalibration—closing underperforming stores, enhancing customer experience, and streamlining operations—heralded a renaissance for Starbucks, reaffirming his legacy not as a static relic but as a beacon of adaptive leadership. Schultz's saga teaches us that leadership, in its most exalted form, is a phoenix capable of rebirth from the ashes of its trials.

In Summation

Leadership, then, is neither eternal nor doomed to obsolescence but exists in a state of perpetual flux, challenged to remain relevant amid the relentless march of change. It beckons leaders to forge legacies not just through the triumphs of today but through the resilience, adaptability, and vision that stand the test of time. As leaders, may we strive not for the immortality of stars but for the enduring impact of the paths we illuminate, guiding those who follow long after our tenure has ended.

Prospecting and Introspecting: Are Leaders Born or Made?

"The greatest leaders are not necessarily the ones who are born with innate qualities, but rather those who embrace the journey of self-discovery and continuous growth." - Warren Bennis

Delving into the perennial debate of leadership's origins, this discourse navigates the nuanced interplay between the inherent and the cultivated, the genetic predisposition, and the experiential sculpting that forges leaders. It is a narrative that transcends the simplicity of being 'born' or 'made,' spotlighting the symbiotic relationship between innate potential and the relentless pursuit of personal evolution.

Unveiling Leadership: Beyond Binary Constructs

Character and Discipline: The Foundation Stones

Leadership, at its core, is an amalgamation of character and discipline. While tales of leaders born with a silver spoon of charisma or decisiveness abound, the essence of true leadership often germinates from the soil of discipline and the relentless pursuit of character refinement. The odyssey of Nelson Mandela exemplifies this blend impeccably. Mandela's resilience, nurtured in the crucible of imprisonment, and his unwavering commitment to justice highlight how leadership is as much about the indomitable spirit as it is about innate qualities.

The Mosaic of Intrinsic and Induced Qualities

Leadership's fabric is woven from both intrinsic threads and those dyed in the hues of experience and learning. Steve Jobs, with his blend of innate ingenuity and a cultivated penchant for innovation, underscores that leadership's brilliance is often kindled by stoking both the natural and the nurtured flames.

Adversity: The Crucible of Leadership

Adversity, with its harsh winds and biting cold, shapes leaders in ways comfort and ease never could. Winston Churchill's leadership, tempered in the fires of world conflict and personal trials, stands as a testament to the resilience and fortitude forged through hardship. His leadership journey illustrates that the crucible of challenge is where the mettle of a leader is truly tested and proven.

The Continuum of Leadership: A Spectrum of Possibilities

Born or Made? The Eternal Inquiry

The discourse on whether leaders are born or made remains vibrant, echoing through the halls of academia and the corridors of corporate power. Yet, this debate might be missing the forest for the trees. Leadership is less about a definitive origin and more about the journey — a continuum where innate potential meets the transformative power of life's experiences.

Prospecting and Introspecting: The Dual Pathways to Leadership

Leadership is a voyage marked by the dual acts of prospecting — seeking out challenges and opportunities for growth — and introspecting, the reflective process of understanding one's inner landscape. This dynamic interplay between outward exploration and inward examination paves the path to true leadership.

Example: Oprah Winfrey — A Paradigm of Emergent Leadership

Oprah Winfrey's narrative beautifully encapsulates the essence of emergent leadership. Rising from adversity with resilience, empathy, and an unwavering resolve to effect change, Oprah's journey from hardship to global influence embodies the convergence of innate predispositions and consciously cultivated abilities. Her leadership transcends the binary of born or made, embodying a spectrum where passion meets purpose, and inherent potential is amplified by relentless growth and self-discovery.

Leadership: A Lifelong Odyssey

Leadership is not a static state achieved at birth or through a series of accomplishments; it is a perpetual odyssey of becoming. It thrives on the continuous interplay between the gifts we are born with and the skills we acquire, between the challenges we seek and the introspection we undertake. Whether leaders are born or made is a question that overlooks the essence of leadership itself — a relentless pursuit of impact, growth, and the ability to inspire and uplift others.

In this realm, every individual holds the potential to lead, to influence, and to leave an indelible mark on the tapestry of humanity. Leadership, then, is an art form — a masterpiece continually evolving, painted on the canvas of life with the brushstrokes of our actions, decisions, and the legacy we aspire to create.

Leadership Styles: Navigating the Weather Patterns

"Leadership is not about predicting the storm but learning to dance in the rain." - Unknown

In the intricate dance of leadership, the rhythm varies widely, akin to the unpredictable patterns of weather that shape our environment. This exploration delves into the essence of leadership styles, comparing them to diverse meteorological phenomena to illuminate their impact on the organizational climate. Through this unique lens, we uncover the characteristics and implications of various leadership approaches, guided by real-life exemplars who have weathered storms and basked in sunlight alike.

The Meteorology of Leadership

The Thunderstorm: Authority in Action Just as a thunderstorm commands the sky with its power and intensity, authoritative leaders take charge with decisiveness and clarity. Winston Churchill, with his indomitable spirit during the darkest hours of World War II, exemplifies this style—his leadership, a beacon of resilience, rallied a nation to stand firm against adversity.

The Gentle Breeze: The Art of Diplomacy

Embodied by leaders like Angela Merkel, the gentle breeze style is all about fostering calm, building consensus, and navigating through challenges with grace. Merkel's tenure as Chancellor of Germany showcased how diplomatic finesse could steer a country through crises, proving that strength often lies in tranquility.

The Tornado: A Whirlwind of Transformation

Elon Musk's leadership mirrors the tornado—dynamic, innovative, and relentlessly pushing the boundaries of what is possible. Musk's ventures, from Tesla's electric cars to SpaceX's rockets, underscore a leadership style marked by visionary zeal and the drive to revolutionize industries.

The Sunshine: Radiating Charisma and Inspiration

Oprah Winfrey, with her magnetic persona and heartfelt eloquence, exemplifies the sunshine style of leadership. Her ability to inspire, motivate, and shine light on critical issues has not only built a media empire but also fostered a global community of empowerment and positive change.

The Fog: Navigating Complexity with Insight

Strategic leaders, akin to navigating through fog, possess the acumen to find clarity amidst uncertainty. Satya Nadella's transformation of Microsoft highlights how strategic foresight and a focus on innovation can guide a tech giant to new heights, even in the densest market fog.

The Rainbow: Celebrating Diversity and Inclusion

Jacinda Ardern's leadership is a vibrant rainbow, embracing diversity and championing inclusivity. Her empathetic approach to governance, prioritizing social justice and equality, illustrates how inclusive leadership can build a cohesive, resilient society.

The Blizzard: The Resilience to Adapt and Overcome

Jeff Bezos, through his journey with Amazon, highlights the blizzard style—adaptable, resilient, and unyielding in the face of change. Bezos's strategic agility has cemented Amazon's place as a behemoth of e-commerce, navigating through market disruptions with the persistence of a relentless snowstorm.

Navigating the Leadership Climate

Understanding the nuances of these leadership styles empowers leaders to adapt their approach to the prevailing organizational climate. Like skilled meteorologists who predict and respond to weather changes, effective leaders assess the environment, anticipate shifts, and adjust their style to lead their teams through any conditions.

Choose Your Climate:

The journey of leadership is not about adhering rigidly to one style but rather about being fluid and adaptable, capable of shifting from the thunderstorm's decisiveness to the gentle breeze's diplomacy as situations demand. The true art lies in recognizing the weather pattern most conducive to nurturing growth, driving change, and achieving success within your organizational ecosystem.

In the ever-changing landscape of leadership, let us learn to dance in the rain, harness the wind, and navigate the fog, embracing the full spectrum of styles to lead with wisdom, courage, and insight.

The Weather Patterns Summary Table

Name of Style	Key Traits	Example
Thunderstorm	Commanding, decisive, assertive, powerful	Winston Churchill, UK
Gentle Breeze	Diplomatic, consensus-building, harmonious	Angela Merkel, Germany
Tornado	Dynamic, visionary, innovative, daring	Elon Musk, Tesla, and SpaceX
Sunshine	Charismatic, inspiring, optimistic, energetic	Oprah Winfrey, Media Mogul
Fog	Strategic, insightful, analytical, visionary	Satya Nadella, Microsoft
Rainbow	Inclusive, diversity-celebrating, empathetic	Jacinda Ardern, New Zealand
Blizzard	Adaptive, resilient, agile, resourceful	Jeff Bezos, Amazon

Leadership: A Personal and Circumstantial Affair

"The measure of a leader is not the absence of failure but the ability to recover from it." - Seth Godin

Leadership, a journey both personal and contextual, defies the one-size-fits-all archetype. This exploration seeks to unravel how leadership's effectiveness is intricately linked to an individual's attributes and the specific circumstances they navigate. Moving beyond the misconception of a universal blueprint for leadership success, we emphasize the critical roles of self-awareness, adaptability, and strategic insight in mastering the art of leadership across varied landscapes.

Leadership Dynamics: A Personal and Circumstantial Symphony

Leadership's essence pulsates through the veins of personal experience, shaped by the unique blend of an individual's traits, background, and the situational challenges they face. The tale of Steve Jobs, with his unparalleled vision yet often contentious leadership style, illustrates how the same qualities that catalyze success in one scenario can evoke strife in another. Leadership, hence, is not about wielding unchecked power but nurturing collective success through collaboration and empathy.

The Dance of Traits and Context

The effectiveness of a leader often hinges on the alignment between their intrinsic qualities and the external environment. Indra Nooyi's tenure at PepsiCo exemplifies how diverse experiences and strategic foresight can navigate complex industry waters, underscoring the importance of wisdom in leadership. Similarly, Satya Nadella's transition at Microsoft highlights how technical prowess, when coupled with empathy, can drive an organization towards innovation and success, even amidst the storms of change.

Leadership: Beyond Role-Playing

Disentangling leadership from the notion of acting or mere role-playing, we assert that genuine leadership is rooted in authenticity, purpose, and tangible impact. Leaders like Malala Yousafzai, through their relentless advocacy and unwavering values, demonstrate that true leadership is about effecting change and inspiring others, far removed from the superficiality of performance.

Leadership's Dual-Edged Sword: Disruption and Unity

Leadership possesses the power to either divide or unite, with a leader's approach significantly influencing organizational harmony. Nelson Mandela's leadership journey, marked by an ethos of reconciliation and unity, showcases how visionary leadership can bridge divides and heal nations. Conversely, figures like Elon Musk embody the disruptive yet unifying force of leadership, challenging the status quo while rallying teams towards a shared vision.

Navigating the Leadership Continuum

In the ever-evolving narrative of leadership, the key to success lies in navigating the delicate balance between personal attributes and the demands of the moment. Leaders must remain fluid, adapting their style and strategies to meet the changing needs of their teams and the wider organizational context.

Abraham Lincoln: A Testament to Resilient Leadership

Abraham Lincoln's life story, marked by persistence through personal and professional setbacks, epitomizes the essence of resilient leadership. His unwavering commitment to his principles, despite numerous failures, and his leadership during one of America's most divisive periods, highlight the profound impact of perseverance, integrity, and moral courage on leadership effectiveness.

Leadership as a Dynamic Journey

Leadership transcends static definitions, thriving on the interplay between an individual's innate predispositions and the dynamic challenges of their environment. It demands a continuous process of learning, self-reflection, and adaptation. By embracing this complex, multifaceted journey, leaders can forge paths that not only lead to personal fulfillment and success but also leave indelible marks on the organizations and communities they serve.

"True Leaders practice to play, play to win, and win with others, not against others." - M. Chahine

Leaders and Leader Makers: The Hidden Architects

"A true leader is not measured by the number of followers they have, but by the number of leaders they create." - Lao Tzu

In the realm of leadership, the architects who shape tomorrow's leaders wield a transformative power often unseen yet profoundly impactful. These mentor figures, or "leader makers," are the bedrock upon which the future of leadership is built. Through their guidance, wisdom, and unwavering support, they craft the leaders of tomorrow, fostering a legacy of growth, empowerment, and innovation.

Unveiling the Architects of Leadership

The Essence of Leader Makers

Leader makers are the unsung heroes behind the scenes, shaping potential into prowess with a blend of mentorship, strategic insight, and personal example. They see beyond the raw material, identifying and nurturing the latent leadership qualities within individuals, guiding them towards realizing their full potential.

The Mentorship Mosaic

In the tapestry of leadership development, mentorship stands out as a vibrant thread. Leader makers provide a compass for navigating the complex landscape of leadership, offering sage advice, constructive feedback, and critical support. They create a safe space for growth, where aspiring leaders can explore their capabilities, challenge their limitations, and refine their vision.

Strategic Development: Crafting Future Leaders

Strategic foresight in leadership development is a hallmark of effective leader makers. They tailor their mentorship to align with both the individual's unique strengths and the evolving needs of the organization. By fostering a diverse pipeline of leadership talent, leader makers ensure that the organization remains resilient, innovative, and forward-looking.

Shadow Leadership: Influence without Limelight

Operating in the background, shadow leaders exert a subtle yet powerful influence on the leadership landscape. Their guidance is like telekinesis—felt but not seen—as they empower emerging leaders to assume responsibility and carve their own paths. This behind-the-scenes mentorship is crucial for cultivating leaders who are confident, autonomous, and ready to lead with integrity.

Celebrating the Impact of Leader Makers

The ripple effect of leader makers is profound, extending far beyond the individuals they mentor. By instilling a culture of leadership development, they not only shape the future of their protégés but also elevate the entire organization, driving sustainable success and fostering an enduring legacy of excellence.

Example: Warren Buffett's Mentorship Legacy

Warren Buffett, the Oracle of Omaha, exemplifies the quintessential leader maker. His mentorship extends across the business spectrum, influencing CEOs, investors, and entrepreneurs with his principles of integrity, long-term investment, and ethical business practices. Buffett's approach to leadership development—rooted in wisdom, patience, and a deep respect for value creation—has inspired a generation of leaders to pursue excellence, make informed decisions, and lead with purpose.

The Human Touch in Leadership Development

Leader makers are the cornerstone of leadership's future, blending human insight with strategic foresight to develop leaders who are not only effective but also empathetic, visionary, and transformative. As we navigate the complexities of the modern world, the role of leader makers becomes ever more crucial, reminding us that at the heart of great leadership lies the profound human connection between mentor and protégé, between the architect and the masterpiece they help to shape.

In honoring leader makers, we acknowledge the profound human element they bring to leadership development, crafting not just leaders but individuals who lead with heart, purpose, and a vision for a better tomorrow.

Leadership Turfs: The Overcrowded Leaderscape

"Conflict arises when the expectations of leaders collide, but resolution emerges when their commitment to the greater good outweighs personal ambitions." - John C. Maxwell

This discourse ventures into the nuanced terrain of shared leadership, probing the dynamics of collaborative leadership models within the realms of organizations and nations. It seeks to illuminate the complexities of a landscape peppered with multiple leaders, pondering the efficacy of such models in propelling entities toward their zenith. Furthermore, it explores the pragmatics of embracing a leadership-rich environment and the pivotal role of individual empowerment in leadership dissemination.

The Coalescence of Leadership: A Synergetic or Chaotic Fusion?

Dual Helms: Navigating Shared Authority

The concept of dual leadership, akin to two captains steering a single ship, invites contemplation on the harmonization of power dynamics and decision-making efficacy. While the potential for innovation and resilience is magnified through collaborative synergy, the shadows of vision discord, role ambiguity, and potential rivalry loom large. Through real-world anecdotes, we dissect the dual-leadership paradigm, unearthing insights into its operational nuances and its ripple effects on organizational harmony.

Harmonizing Diverse Leadership Styles

The orchestration of complementary leadership styles offers a strategic palette for enriching the leadership narrative within teams. This approach leverages the diverse array of strengths, perspectives, and methodologies that leaders bring to the table, aiming to enhance collective problem-solving and goal attainment. The challenge lies in ensuring these leadership forces attract rather than repel, creating a cohesive unit that thrives on mutual support and shared aspirations.

The Dynamics of Leadership Density

The trend of hiring and gathering leadership talent en masse – reads "hoarding" - sparks a dialogue on the essence of leadership and its distribution within the corporate echelon. This section scrutinizes the balance between leadership abundance and its potential to dilute the essence of leadership itself, advocating for a mindful approach to leadership cultivation that values depth over breadth.

Empowering the Leader Within

At the heart of dynamic leadership landscapes lies the principle of empowerment, recognizing the potential within every individual to exhibit leadership, irrespective of their official title or position. This philosophy champions the idea of decentralized leadership, where initiative, creativity, and ownership are dispersed across the organization, fostering an environment were leadership flourishes organically.

Leadership Turfs: The Choreography of Cohesion and Individuality

The play of leadership within crowded arenas necessitates a choreography that balances individual prowess with collective synchronization. Organizations and leaders alike must navigate this intricate mix, embracing the diversity of leadership while steering towards unified objectives.

Example: The Apple Dichotomy

The historical tussle between Steve Jobs and John Sculley at Apple epitomizes the challenges and revelations born from leadership clashes. Their divergent leadership styles — Jobs' revolutionary zeal juxtaposed with Sculley's conservative stewardship — catalyzed a period of turmoil and transformation within Apple. This narrative not only underscores the potential friction inherent in shared leadership scenarios but also highlights the evolutionary push such dynamics can provide, propelling organizations to introspect, adapt, and soar to new heights.

Leading Amidst Leadership

The quest for effective leadership in a realm abundant with leaders is both a challenge and an opportunity. It calls for a nuanced understanding of leadership dynamics, a commitment to fostering leadership at every level, and a willingness to embrace the diversity of leadership styles. As we tread this complex landscape, let us strive for a leadership ethos that values unity, adaptability, and the collective pursuit of excellence, ensuring that even in crowded spaces, every leader has the latitude to shine and the platform to contribute to the greater narrative of success.

The Strategic Pause: The Unseen Power in Leadership

"In the realm of leadership, the true art often lies not in the flurry of actions but in the strategic pause, the deliberate choice to observe, understand, and then navigate the terrain you aim to conquer." - Unknown

In the fervor of stepping into leadership roles, the immediate impulse to act, to highlight decisiveness, is a common trap that ensnares many. Yet, amidst the cacophony of expectations and the rush towards visible achievements, lies the unheralded wisdom of patience — the choice to pause, reflect, and absorb before leaping into the fray.

Embracing the Strategic Pause

The notion that effective leadership necessitates instantaneous results is a fallacy that disregards the nuanced tapestry of organizational dynamics. The strategic pause — a period dedicated to observation, learning, and meticulous planning — is not inaction but a profound action in itself. It is in these moments of seeming stillness that leaders can distill clarity from chaos, forging a path forward that is informed, deliberate, and resilient.

The Virtue of Patience in Leadership

The adage that rectifying the blunders made in haste during the initial phase of leadership can consume upwards of a year underscores the quintessential role of patience. This period of acclimatization is not merely about biding time but about cultivating an intimate understanding of the organizational ethos, its people, and the myriad challenges and opportunities that lie within.

The Power of Observation and Strategic Planning

In the early days of leadership, the temptation to embark on a whirlwind of change can be overwhelming. Yet, the leaders who stand the test of time are those who recognize the power of observation, the insights gleaned from listening, and the strength found in strategic planning. This approach not only fortifies the leader's foundation but also engenders trust and respect among team members, who see a leader committed to thoughtful and informed decision-making.

Illustrating Patience and Strategy: The Best Buy Turnaround

Hubert Joly's stewardship of Best Buy encapsulates the essence of strategic patience. At a juncture when Best Buy grappled with existential threats from digital behemoths and shifting consumer landscapes, Joly chose not to rush into precipitous action. Instead, he embarked on a deliberate journey of understanding — immersing himself in the company's core, connecting with employees, customers, and stakeholders, and identifying the unique strengths that could be leveraged for revival.

Joly's strategy hinged on enhancing the in-store experience, digital integration, and a relentless focus on customer satisfaction. This patient, calculated approach not only resurrected Best Buy from the brink of obsolescence but also redefined its market position, showcasing the transformative power of leadership that values the strategic pause.

The Art of Strategic Leadership

The journey of leadership is punctuated not by the steps taken in haste but by those measured with thought, understanding, and strategic insight. The strategic pause, far from being a sign of indecision, is a testament to a leader's strength, foresight, and commitment to sustainable success.

In the tapestry of leadership, patience is not merely a virtue but a strategic tool, enabling leaders to navigate the complexities of their roles with wisdom, clarity, and a vision that transcends the immediacy of action for the profundity of impact.

Harnessing Leadership Spikes: The Essence of Transformational Influence

"Success in leadership often comes from amplifying your strengths rather than fixing your weaknesses." - Marcus Buckingham

Leadership, in its most impactful form, is not merely about the balance of skills but the elevation of innate strengths to levels of extraordinary influence. These standout traits, or Leadership Spikes, are the unique qualities that differentiate transformative leaders from the rest. This exploration delves into the concept of Leadership Spikes, examining how these potent attributes can be strategically harnessed to magnify leadership effectiveness and drive organizational success.

Deciphering Leadership Spikes

Leadership Spikes transcend ordinary leadership attributes, marking the points where a leader's capabilities reach their zenith. These spikes could range from unparalleled resilience and visionary foresight to exceptional communication and innovation prowess. Identifying and nurturing these spikes enables leaders to channel their energies where they can make the most significant impact, transforming potential into palpable success.

Strategic Amplification of Leadership Spikes

The art of leadership lies not in a quest for perfection across all fronts but in the strategic amplification of one's most potent traits. Leaders can achieve remarkable outcomes by focusing on enhancing their inherent strengths while managing their weaknesses. This strategic approach involves recognizing one's spikes and crafting a leadership narrative that leverages these strengths to inspire, motivate, and lead effectively.

Complementary and Supplementary Spikes

Leadership effectiveness can be significantly enhanced through the strategic combination of complementary and supplementary spikes. Complementary spikes bridge gaps in a leader's skill set, providing a well-rounded approach to leadership challenges. In contrast, supplementary spikes bolster existing strengths, enabling leaders to excel in their areas of expertise and push the boundaries of innovation and influence.

Cultivating a Synergistic Team Environment

The true potential of Leadership Spikes is unlocked not in isolation but through the collective synergy of a team. Leaders must surround themselves with individuals whose spikes complement their own, creating a dynamic team capable of tackling diverse challenges with creativity and resilience. This environment fosters mutual growth, innovation, and a shared commitment to achieving common goals, propelling the organization forward.

Empowering Leaders Through Strategic Focus

The journey of leveraging Leadership Spikes is a testament to the transformative power of focused leadership development. By embracing their unique strengths and strategically aligning their efforts with organizational goals, leaders can navigate the complexities of their roles with confidence and clarity, driving impactful change and leaving a legacy.

Example: The Visionary Leadership of Jeff Bezos

Jeff Bezos, the visionary founder of Amazon, exemplifies the profound impact of harnessing Leadership Spikes. Bezos' foresight in recognizing the potential of the internet for retail revolutionized the industry, creating a global e-commerce giant. His relentless pursuit of innovation, customer obsession, and resilience in the face of setbacks transformed Amazon into a behemoth that continually redefines market standards. Bezos' leadership journey underscores the power of focusing on one's spikes to achieve exponential success and enduring influence. Bezos was after all a great leader who knew very well how to put even a greater team behind his vision and goals.

The Art of Elevating Leadership

In the realm of leadership, the strategic elevation of one's innate spikes is the cornerstone of transformative influence. It is through the focused enhancement of these unique strengths that leaders can inspire their teams, drive organizational success, and carve paths that others aspire to follow. In embracing and amplifying their Leadership Spikes, leaders not only achieve personal fulfillment but also catalyze positive change that resonates across the broader landscape of their industries and beyond.

The Paragon of Leadership: In Search of the Uber Leader

"Excellence is never an accident; it is always the result of high intention, sincere effort, intelligent direction, and skillful execution." – Aristotle

The Ideal of Leadership Excellence

In the intricate tapestry of leadership, there emerges the concept of the Paragon Leader, akin to the philosophical ideal of the Philosopher King. These individuals are emblematic of leadership at its zenith, embodying a blend of profound intellectual depth, unwavering ethical standards, and an indomitable spirit of service.

Dedication to Excellence

For the Paragon Leader, leadership transcends mere responsibility—it is an earnest commitment to fostering excellence in every action and decision. Their journey is not motivated by personal accolades but by a deep-seated desire to effectuate positive change and uphold the highest echelons of moral and ethical conduct.

Unyielding Work Ethic and Purpose

Characterized by an exceptional work ethic, the Paragon Leader's endeavors are propelled by a clear sense of purpose that extends beyond personal ambitions to encompass the well-being and advancement of the collective. Their leadership is a manifestation of service, a relentless pursuit to contribute value and inspire greatness in others.

Conviction and Courage

Possessing a robust conviction in their values, Paragon Leaders stand as pillars of integrity, even in solitude, championing their beliefs with courage and resilience. They view leadership not as a position of power but as a platform for principled advocacy and transformative action.

Resilience Amidst Trials

Faced with adversity, the Paragon Leader exhibits unmatched resilience, transforming challenges into catalysts for growth and strengthening their resolve. They embrace setbacks as integral to the leadership odyssey, each obstacle a stepping stone toward greater wisdom and fortitude.

The Humble Journey

The essence of the Paragon Leader lies not in titles or temporal achievements but in the indelible impact they imprint on the hearts and minds of those they lead. Leadership, for them, is a perpetual voyage of growth, humility, and gratitude.

The Quintessence of Leadership

The Paragon Leader stands as a testament to the pinnacle of leadership excellence, a beacon illuminating the path to virtuous and purpose-driven leadership. While the archetype of the Uber Leader may be a rarefied ideal, it underscores the profound potential of leadership that is rooted in ethical principles, intellectual depth, and a commitment to the collective good.

In celebrating the ethos of the Paragon Leader, we are reminded that true leadership is not measured by the breadth of one's power but by the depth of one's influence, the strength of one's character, and the capacity to inspire and elevate those around us.

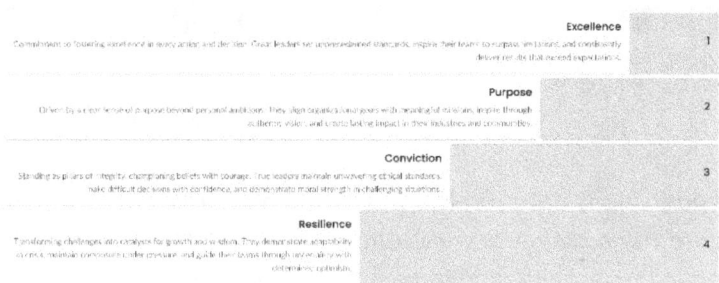

A Tribute to Aspirational Leadership

In homage to the concept of aspirational leadership, it is essential to acknowledge that while the Paragon Leader may represent an ideal, the essence of their leadership qualities is accessible to all who are committed to the journey of self-improvement, ethical governance, and service to others. The narrative of the Paragon Leader inspires us to strive for excellence, to lead with integrity, and to leave a legacy defined by the positive impact we have on the world. In this spirit, we are all encouraged to seek, recognize, and embody the traits of the Paragon Leader in our daily lives, fostering an environment where leadership is synonymous with growth, service, and unwavering commitment to the greater good.

Navigating the Economy of Leadership: Investments and Returns

"Leadership is not merely a position but an economic exchange, where the currency is trust, effort, vision, and the dividends are innovation, growth, and impact." - Adapted from Warren Buffett

In the intricate dance of leadership, the dynamics extend beyond mere guidance and direction to encompass a nuanced economic exchange. This exchange involves a complex interplay of investments, expectations, outcomes, and value, each component integral to the leadership narrative and its influence on stakeholders and organizational landscapes.

The Economics of Leadership: A Four-Dimensional Analysis

Investing in Leadership: The Stakeholder's Commitment

The economy of leadership begins with the stakeholder's investment, which is not limited to financial capital but includes trust, loyalty, support, and effort. This foundational investment lays the groundwork for effective leadership, setting the stage for a mutual exchange aimed at achieving shared goals and visions.

The Leadership Proposition: Defining Expectations

The 'ask' of leadership encapsulates the leader's vision, objectives, and the prerequisites for achieving them. It is a clarion call to stakeholders, outlining what is expected of them and what they, in turn, can anticipate from their leader. This proposition sets the expectations, delineates the scope of engagement, and galvanizes collective effort towards a common objective.

Pricing Leadership: Measuring Outcomes and Benefits

The 'price' of leadership reflects the tangible and intangible returns on the stakeholder's investment. It is the measure of leadership's effectiveness, gauged through the realization of goals, the advancement of the organization, and the broader impact on the community. This dimension assesses the direct and indirect benefits derived from leadership actions and decisions, serving as a barometer for leadership value.

Valuing Leadership: The Cumulative Impact

The value of leadership transcends immediate outcomes, embodying the lasting momentum and potential catalyzed through effective leadership practices. It encompasses the broader, long-term benefits to the organization, its people, and the society at large, including innovation, cultural enrichment, and societal advancement. The value of leadership is the ultimate metric of its significance and legacy, offering a holistic view of its contribution to shaping a better future.

Balancing the Leadership Ledger: Costs, Asks, Prices, and Values

The leadership economy is governed by a delicate balance between what is invested, asked, priced, and valued. Effective leaders navigate this balance with acuity, ensuring that the investments made by stakeholders are met with meaningful returns, both in the immediate and the long term. This balance fosters trust, drives engagement, and cultivates a culture of mutual respect and shared success.

Example: The Strategic Stewardship of Jeff Weiner

Jeff Weiner's tenure as CEO of LinkedIn exemplifies the principles of leadership economics in action. Faced with competitive pressures and the challenge of monetizing a growing platform, Weiner spearheaded strategic initiatives that required significant upfront investment but delivered substantial value to LinkedIn and its stakeholders. Through product innovation, a focus on data analytics, and a commitment to culture and employee well-being, Weiner's leadership not only propelled LinkedIn to new heights of success but also cemented its reputation as a pioneering and trusted professional network.

The Enduring Economy of Effective Leadership

The economy of leadership is a testament to the transformative power of strategic, value-driven leadership. By understanding and effectively managing the economic dimensions of leadership—costs, asks, prices, and values—leaders can inspire confidence, foster innovation, and leave a lasting impact. The leadership economy is not about the accumulation of wealth or status but about the generation of value that transcends the individual and enriches the collective fabric of our organizations and societies.

The Economic of Leadership in Tabular Form

Aspect	Definition
Cost of Leadership	The resources, trust, loyalty, and support invested by stakeholders for effective leadership.
Ask of Leadership	The expectations and requirements that leaders articulate for themselves and stakeholders.
Price of Leadership	The outcomes and benefits received by stakeholders in return for their contributions.
Value of Leadership	The overall potential or momentum of tangible and intangible benefits resulting from effective leadership.

Section 2: A Crash Course - Private Equity 101

The What and Who of Private Equity:

Part 1: Private Equity -- The Industry
Part 2: Private Equity -- The Players

Part 1: Private Equity - The Industry

What Is Private Equity?

Investing in Private Companies
Private companies typically raise funds by issuing shares through a private placement to a select group of institutional or individual investors who meet certain requirements for wealth, income, or financial knowledge. These shares do not trade on public exchanges.

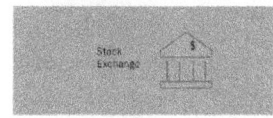

A Primer on Private Equity – The Primal yet Obscure Asset Class

Private Equity (PE) represents a sophisticated and dynamic sector of the financial world, offering unique opportunities for investors to engage directly with their investments. This chapter introduces the foundational elements of PE, illuminating its role, strategies, and the profound impact it has on the global investment landscape.

Why Private Equity?

Enhanced Returns and Active Ownership PE stands out for its potential to generate superior returns through direct involvement in portfolio companies. This active ownership model empowers investors to influence strategic decisions, driving significant value creation beyond what is typically achievable in public markets.

Diversification PE investments diversify investors' portfolios, mitigating risks associated with traditional asset classes. By venturing into various industries and regions, PE provides a hedge against market volatility and enhances the overall investment performance.

Long-Term Perspective Unlike the short-term focus prevalent in public markets, PE embodies a long-term investment philosophy. This approach aligns investor and company goals, fostering environments where businesses can flourish over extended periods.

Asset Class Overview

1. Venture Capital (VC) VC focuses on funding innovative startups with the potential for exponential growth, playing a crucial role in the development of innovative technologies and business models.

2. Growth Equity This strategy supports established companies at the cusp of rapid expansion, providing the capital necessary to scale operations and enter new markets.

3. Buyouts PE firms often acquire mature companies through buyouts, implementing operational efficiencies and strategic improvements to unlock latent value.

4. Special Situations Investments in distressed assets and companies facing unique challenges represent opportunities for PE firms to capitalize on market inefficiencies and drive turnaround successes.

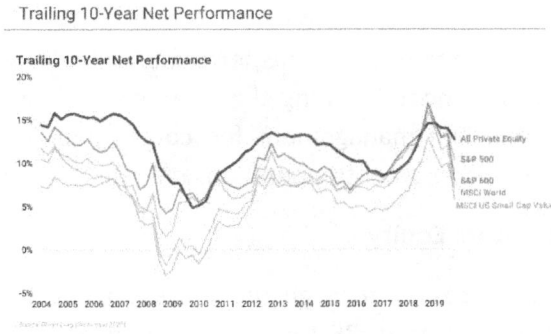

The Private Equity Process

From origination to realization, the PE investment process is a meticulous journey designed to maximize value at every stage. It begins with identifying promising opportunities, conducting thorough due diligence, and executing deals with precision. The subsequent value creation phase is pivotal, as PE firms work closely with portfolio companies to implement transformative strategies. Ultimately, the realization phase focuses on executing profitable exit strategies, ensuring substantial returns for investors.

Private Equity Fund Structure

PE funds can be either open-end or closed end, with a typical lifecycle that includes a mandate defining the investment strategy, a hurdle rate setting the performance benchmark, and a carried interest model aligning the interests of fund managers and investors. The management fee covers operational costs, ensuring the fund's smooth operation.

Access to Private Equity

Investors can access PE through direct investments in companies, primary investments in PE funds, or secondary markets. Each avenue offers distinct levels of control, risk, and potential returns, catering to the diverse preferences of investors.

Private Equity is a nuanced and powerful asset class that demands a deep understanding of its mechanisms, strategies, and inherent risks. By providing an initial overview of PE, this chapter lays the groundwork for exploring the complex yet rewarding world of private equity investing. The subsequent chapters will delve deeper into each aspect, offering readers comprehensive insights into mastering the art of PE investing.

Understanding Private Equity

Private Equity (PE) stands as a cornerstone of the investment world, offering a blend of strategic capital, active management, and the pursuit of transformative growth. At its heart, PE embodies the partnership between investors and companies, aiming not just for financial gain but for the evolution and scaling of businesses across sectors. This exploration delves into the rationale behind PE investments, highlighting their distinctive approach to fostering innovation, driving performance, and achieving long-term value creation.

Why Private Equity?

PE attracts investors with the promise of not only enhanced returns but also the opportunity for significant, direct impact on business strategy and growth. This active investment model grants investors a seat at the table, allowing them to steer companies towards achieving their full potential. Moreover, PE's emphasis on long-term investment horizons aligns with the developmental needs of businesses, providing them with the runway to implement substantial, value-adding changes.

Asset Class Overview

The landscape of PE is diverse, encompassing various investment strategies tailored to various stages of a company's lifecycle. From the high-risk, high-reward world of Venture Capital, funding nascent startups with groundbreaking ideas, to the strategic maneuvers of Buyouts and Special Situations, PE covers a broad spectrum of investment philosophies. Each strategy reflects a different facet of PE's overarching goal: to unlock and enhance value wherever possible.

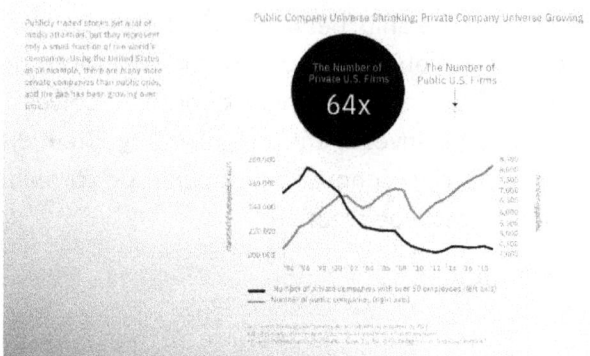

The Size of the Private Equity Opportunity

The Private Equity Process

The journey through a PE investment, from origination to exit, is a meticulous and strategic endeavor. It begins with the identification of potential investments and extends through detailed due diligence, deal execution, and active management, culminating in a carefully planned exit strategy. This process is characterized by a deep engagement with the portfolio company, leveraging PE firms' expertise to drive operational improvements, strategic redirection, and growth acceleration.

As we navigate the nuances of Private Equity, it becomes clear that this asset class is not just about financial investment but about partnership, strategy, and a shared vision for growth and success. PE offers a unique blend of risk and reward, challenging investors, and companies alike to push the boundaries of what is possible in the business world.

The Private Equity Process

The Private Equity Process encapsulates a series of strategic steps designed to identify, evaluate, acquire, manage, and exit investments with the goal of generating high returns for investors. This comprehensive journey is both methodical and dynamic, tailored to unlock the potential within companies and drive substantial growth.

Identification and Sourcing

The journey begins with the meticulous process of identifying promising investment opportunities. This involves leveraging networks, industry expertise, and rigorous market analysis to find companies that align with the PE firm's investment criteria and strategic vision.

Due Diligence

Once a potential investment is identified, a thorough due diligence process ensues. This critical phase involves deep dives into the company's financials, operations, market position, and competitive landscape. The aim is to uncover every risk and opportunity, shaping the investment thesis and valuation.

Deal Structuring and Execution

With due diligence complete, the deal moves into the structuring and execution phase. This step involves negotiating terms, finalizing the investment structure, and legally securing the transaction. Creative financial engineering is often employed to optimize returns and mitigate risks.

Value Creation

Post-acquisition, the focus shifts to value creation. Through operational improvements, strategic guidance, and leveraging industry trends, PE firms actively work to enhance the company's performance. This often involves implementing modern technologies, expanding into new markets, and optimizing financial practices.

Investment Process

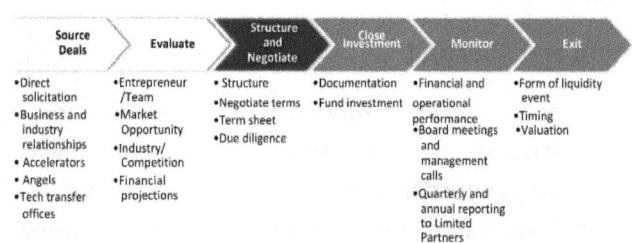

Exit Strategy

The final phase of the Private Equity process is the exit, where the PE firm seeks to sell its stake in the company at a significant profit. Common exit strategies include public offerings, sales to strategic buyers, or secondary sales to other investment firms. The exit is meticulously planned to maximize returns and often involves preparing the company for the transition, ensuring a sustainable future beyond PE ownership.

Throughout this journey, the Private Equity process is characterized by a blend of strategic foresight, financial acumen, and operational expertise. Each step is executed with the dual objectives of fostering company growth and ensuring lucrative returns for the PE firm's investors, making Private Equity a unique and impactful component of the global investment landscape.

Private Equity Fund Structure

The structure of Private Equity (PE) funds is integral to the operational dynamics and investment strategy of the asset class. Understanding this structure is essential for investors and professionals navigating the PE landscape.

Open-End and Closed-End Funds

PE funds typically operate as closed-end funds with a fixed term, usually 10 to 12 years. This contrasts with open-end funds, which have no set expiration and allow for ongoing investment and redemption. The closed-end structure of PE funds aligns with the long-term investment horizon needed to realize value in portfolio companies.

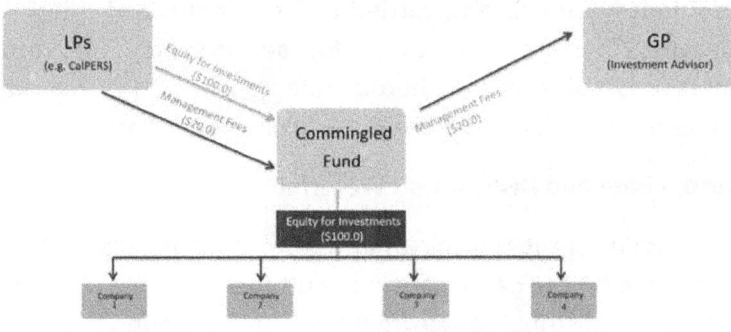

- Assumes a $120MM commitment as an LP to a 10 year fund.
- Terms: Average management fee of ~2% per year for the life of the fund and 20% profit share with GP.
- Assumes no preferred return.

Fund Organization and Operations

A PE fund is structured around a partnership model, with the PE firm acting as the General Partner (GP) responsible for managing the fund and making investment decisions. Investors in the fund, known as Limited Partners (LPs), provide the capital but have limited involvement in the day-to-day management.

Investment Mandate and Strategies

Each PE fund operates under a specific mandate, detailing the fund's investment focus, geographic preference, industry sectors, and risk profile. This mandate guides the GP in selecting and managing investments that align with the fund's objectives.

Management Fees and Carried Interest

PE funds charge management fees, typically around 1.5% to 2% of the committed capital annually, to cover operational costs. Additionally, GPs receive carried interest, a share of the profits (usually 20%), as an incentive for performance. The carried interest is subject to a hurdle rate, ensuring LPs receive a predetermined return before the GP collects its share.

Hurdle Rate and Distribution Waterfall

The hurdle rate is the minimum return that must be achieved before the GP can participate in the profits. Once this rate is met, profits are distributed according to the distribution waterfall, detailing the order in which returns are allocated between LPs and the GP.

Access and Participation

Access to PE funds is typically reserved for institutional investors, high-net-worth individuals, and family offices due to the high minimum investment requirements and the illiquid nature of the investments. However, the landscape is evolving, with new platforms and fund structures providing broader access to PE investments.

PE funds' structured approach enables them to undertake significant investments, drive strategic improvements, and generate substantial returns for their stakeholders. The fund structure is pivotal in aligning the interests of GPs and LPs, ensuring both parties are motivated towards the success of the fund's investments.

Access to Private Equity

Gaining access to Private Equity (PE) presents unique opportunities and challenges for investors looking to diversify their portfolios and engage in direct investments. Here is an overview of the main avenues through which investors can participate in the PE landscape.

Direct Investment

Direct investment allows investors to take an active role by directly acquiring stakes in private companies. This method appeals to investors seeking to have a hands-on approach in managing their investments and influencing company strategies. However, it requires significant capital, expertise, and due diligence capabilities.

Funds of Funds

Funds of funds offer a way to invest in PE by pooling resources to invest in multiple PE funds. This approach provides diversification across different funds, strategies, and geographic regions, lowering the risk associated with individual fund investments. It is an accessible option for investors with limited capital or those new to the PE space.

Co-Investment

Co-investment opportunities arise when investors directly invest alongside a PE fund in a specific deal. This allows investors to bypass the fund structure, reducing fees and gaining exposure to specific investments. Co-investments require strong relationships with PE firms and the ability to quickly assess and commit to deals.

Secondary Market

The secondary market for PE provides liquidity by allowing investors to buy and sell existing commitments in PE funds. This avenue is attractive for investors looking to adjust their investment exposure or timing without the long lock-up periods typical of PE investments.

Crowdfunding Platforms

Emerging crowdfunding platforms offer retail and accredited investors access to early-stage investment opportunities traditionally reserved for VC and PE firms. These platforms democratize access to PE, allowing for smaller investment minimums and increased transparency.

Listed Private Equity

Some PE firms are publicly traded, allowing investors to gain exposure to PE through the purchase of publicly listed shares. This option combines the liquidity of public markets with the potential returns of PE investments.

Navigating the avenues of access to PE requires an understanding of the intricacies of each option, including the associated risks, costs, and potential returns. Investors should carefully consider their investment objectives, risk tolerance, and the operational capabilities of PE firms before committing capital to this asset class.

PE Lifecycle and Mechanisms

The lifecycle of a Private Equity (PE) investment is a complex journey that spans from the initial investment to the eventual exit, encompassing various stages and mechanisms designed to maximize value creation and return on investment. Understanding these stages and the underlying mechanisms is crucial for both investors and practitioners within the PE landscape.

Initial Investment and Capital Commitment

The lifecycle begins with the PE firm identifying and evaluating potential investment opportunities. Once a suitable target is identified, the firm commits capital to acquire a stake in the company, often through a combination of equity and debt financing. This stage requires thorough due diligence to assess the viability and potential of the investment.

Value Creation Strategies

After securing the investment, the focus shifts to value creation. PE firms employ a range of strategies to improve the performance and profitability of the portfolio company. These may include operational improvements, strategic repositioning, cost reduction initiatives, and revenue growth strategies. The aim is to enhance the company's value over the investment period, typically ranging from 4 to 7 years.

Monitoring and Governance

Throughout the investment period, PE firms actively monitor the performance of the portfolio company, providing strategic guidance and support. This involves regular assessments of financial performance, operational efficiency, and strategic progress. Effective governance is established through board representation, ensuring that the PE firm can influence key decisions and drive the implementation of value creation initiatives.

Exit Strategies

The final stage of the PE lifecycle involves exiting the investment to realize returns. Common exit strategies include an Initial Public Offering (IPO), sale to a strategic buyer, sale to another PE firm (secondary buyout), or recapitalization. The choice of exit strategy depends on market conditions, the maturity of the business, and the investment objectives of the PE firm.

Mechanisms for Value Realization

Several mechanisms facilitate the realization of value from PE investments. These include:

- **Leveraged Buyouts (LBOs):** Using significant amounts of debt to finance the purchase of a company, aiming to pay down the debt over time and sell the company at a higher valuation.

- **Growth Capital:** Investing in more mature companies to finance expansion, new product development, or restructuring, without changing control of the business.
- **Distressed Investments:** Acquiring stakes in financially troubled companies with the aim of turning them around through operational improvements and financial restructuring.

Exit Strategies: Maximizing Value

1. **IPO** — High returns, brand recognition
2. **Strategic Sale** — Faster exit, industry synergy
3. **Secondary Buyout** — Cash liquidity, quick turnaround
4. **Recapitalization** — Partial exit, retain control

Each exit strategy offers unique advantages and challenges. The key to success lies in aligning the chosen approach with market conditions, portfolio company goals, and investor preferences.

The lifecycle and mechanisms of PE investments underscore the hands-on, active management approach characteristic of private equity. By strategically navigating each stage of the lifecycle and effectively employing various mechanisms for value realization, PE firms aim to deliver substantial returns to their investors, contributing to the dynamism and growth of the companies they invest in.

Valuation in Private Equity

Valuation is a cornerstone of Private Equity (PE), providing a systematic approach to determining the worth of companies within the PE portfolio. This process is vital, not just at the acquisition stage but throughout the lifecycle of the investment, influencing decisions related to capital injection, strategic pivots, and eventual exits. Given the private nature of these companies, valuation poses unique challenges, necessitating a blend of art and science to navigate the complexities involved.

Key Valuation Methods in PE

- **Discounted Cash Flow (DCF):** This method forecasts the investee company's future cash flows and discounts them back to their present value, considering the risk associated with achieving those cash flows. DCF is particularly useful for companies with predictable, stable cash flows.

- **Comparable Analysis:** This involves evaluating the company against publicly traded companies or recent transactions within the same industry. Metrics such as price-to-earnings (P/E) ratios, Enterprise Value/EBITDA, and others are used to derive valuation multiples.

- **Leveraged Buyout (LBO) Analysis:** This approach assesses the potential returns a PE firm can achieve through the acquisition of the company using significant levels of debt financing. The focus is on the investee's ability to generate cash flow sufficient to service the debt and provide an attractive return on equity.

Adjustments and Considerations

Valuation in PE is not a static exercise; it requires periodic adjustments and reassessments to reflect the company's evolving financial health, market conditions, and the impact of strategic initiatives undertaken by the PE firm. Additionally, considerations such as market comparability, industry trends, and regulatory changes play a critical role in ensuring the valuation remains relevant and accurate.

The Role of Valuation in Investment Decision-Making

Accurate valuation is essential for making informed investment decisions, from identifying attractive investment opportunities to executing timely exits. It helps PE firms assess the risk-return profile of their investments, allocate capital efficiently, and develop strategies to enhance value.

Risks and Disadvantages of Private Equity

Illiquidity
- Private equity investments are illiquid and cannot be easily entered or exited. Once invested in a business, stakeholders are generally locked in until a realization event occurs

Complex Structure
- When investing in a private equity fund, the investment is called down in tranches for specific uses, with distributions coming unpredictably. Given the more complex cash flows, increased infrastructure is required to manage these investments. Page 7 offers an illustration of the investor's potential cash flows

Valuation Reporting
- Unlike public investments, private companies are only valued once per quarter and marks do not come out until months after quarter-end. These marks are also harder to independently validate

Blind Pool
- When committing to a new private equity fund, the companies in which the fund will invest is not determined in advance

High Fees
- Private equity fund managers charge higher fees than other asset classes. The standard fee structure for many funds is an annual 2% management fee, as well as a 20% fee on all profits generated by the fund

Business Risk
- Private equity fund portfolio companies are often smaller and/or less mature than public companies – particularly those early in their lifecycle. These companies also often have other complexities threatening the success of the business that are not as prevalent in companies that are public

Challenges in PE Valuation

- **Lack of Public Information:** Private companies do not have the same disclosure requirements as public companies, making it difficult to obtain detailed financial data.

- **Subjectivity:** Many assumptions underpin valuation models, including growth rates, discount rates, and exit multiples. These assumptions can introduce a degree of subjectivity into the valuation process.

- **Market Volatility:** Fluctuations in market conditions can significantly impact valuation, especially for companies in volatile sectors.

Despite these challenges, valuation remains an indispensable tool in the PE toolkit, enabling firms to navigate the investment landscape with a clear understanding of the value creation potential of their portfolio companies. As the PE industry continues to evolve, so too will the methodologies and approaches to valuation, ensuring they remain aligned with the dynamic nature of the investments they seek to appraise.

Fees and the J-Curve

In the realm of Private Equity (PE), understanding the financial intricacies, particularly fees and the J-Curve effect, is crucial for investors seeking to navigate this asset class successfully. These elements not only influence the overall returns but also shed light on the temporal nature of investments and the associated cost structures that govern PE funds.

Fees in Private Equity

PE funds typically levy two main types of fees: management fees and performance fees, often referred to as carried interest.

- **Management Fees:** These are charged annually as a percentage of either the committed capital or the net asset value (NAV) of the fund, ranging typically from 1.5% to 2%. They cover the operational costs of managing the fund, including salaries, office expenses, and due diligence activities.

- **Carried Interest:** This is a performance fee that aligns the interests of the fund managers with those of the investors. It is usually set at 20% of the fund's profits, subject to the fund surpassing a predefined hurdle rate or return threshold. This ensures that fund managers are rewarded for generating substantial returns for their investors.

The J-Curve Effect

The J-Curve effect is a distinctive pattern observed in the return profile of PE investments. It illustrates the initial period of negative returns followed by a significant uptick as investments mature and begin to yield profits.

- **Initial Investment Phase:** In the early years, the fund incurs expenses related to acquiring and managing portfolio companies, leading to negative returns. This phase corresponds to the downward slope of the J-Curve.

- **Value Creation and Exit Phase:** As portfolio companies grow and operational improvements take effect, the fund starts realizing gains from successful exits, such as IPOs, trade sales, or secondary sales. This period of positive returns represents the upward slope of the J-Curve.

The J-Curve: A Fundamental Concept in PE

1. **Initial Losses**
   PE investments often start with negative returns due to transaction and integration costs.

2. **Turnaround**
   Portfolio companies stabilize and begin showing positive performance trends.

3. **Growth Phase**
   Value creation initiatives drive substantial gains in the portfolio's worth.

4. **Exit Profits**
   Successful exits yield high returns, culminating the J-Curve's upward trajectory.

Implications for Investors

Understanding the J-Curve effect is pivotal for investors, as it sets realistic expectations for the timing of returns. It underscores the importance of patience and a long-term investment horizon in PE. Additionally, the structure of fees emphasizes the need for investors to select fund managers with a proven track record of generating returns that justify the costs.

Navigating the Costs

For investors, it is essential to conduct thorough due diligence on the fee structure and performance history of PE funds. Evaluating past J-Curve patterns can provide insights into a fund manager's effectiveness in navigating the initial challenging phase and successfully executing value-creating strategies.

In summary, fees and the J-Curve are integral components of the PE investment landscape. They encapsulate the cost of access to high-caliber investment management and the temporal dynamics of returns, respectively. For both seasoned and prospective PE investors, a comprehensive understanding of these concepts is indispensable for making informed decisions and optimizing investment outcomes in the complex yet rewarding domain of Private Equity.

Risks in Private Equity

Navigating the investment landscape of Private Equity (PE) entails a keen understanding of its inherent risks. While the potential for high returns is a significant draw for investors, the unique characteristics of PE investments introduce specific risk factors that must be carefully managed.

Equity Risk

PE investments are subject to equity risk, reflecting the volatility in the value of investments due to market fluctuations and economic conditions. The performance of portfolio companies within a PE fund can be significantly impacted by broader economic trends, regulatory changes, and industry-specific developments. Mitigating equity risk involves thorough due diligence, diversification across sectors, and strategic timing of entry and exit.

Liquidity Risk

A defining characteristic of PE is the illiquidity of investments. Unlike public markets, where securities can be bought and sold with relative ease, PE investments are typically locked in for several years. This illiquidity risk means that investors may not be able to quickly convert their investments into cash without potentially incurring losses. Strategies to manage liquidity risk include ensuring sufficient liquidity buffers within an investment portfolio and aligning investment horizons with liquidity needs.

Operational Risk

Operational risk in PE relates to the challenges associated with managing and growing portfolio companies. This can include execution risks, competitive pressures, and operational inefficiencies. PE firms mitigate operational risk by actively engaging with management teams, providing strategic guidance, and leveraging industry expertise to drive operational improvements.

Leverage Risk

Leveraged Buyouts (LBOs), a common PE strategy, involve using significant amounts of debt to finance the acquisition of companies. While leverage can amplify returns, it also increases the risk of financial distress, particularly in adverse market conditions or if the portfolio company underperforms. Managing leverage risk requires careful capital structure optimization, prudent use of debt, and robust cash flow management.

Regulatory and Compliance Risk

PE firms and their portfolio companies must navigate a complex regulatory environment that can vary significantly across jurisdictions. Changes in regulations, tax laws, and compliance requirements pose risks that can impact the viability of investment strategies and the legal standing of investments. Continuous monitoring of the regulatory landscape and adherence to compliance best practices are essential for mitigating these risks.

Exit Risk

The success of a PE investment is often contingent on executing a successful exit strategy, such as an IPO, sale to a strategic buyer, or secondary sale. Exit risk encompasses the uncertainties associated with finding a suitable exit opportunity that maximizes returns for investors. Effective exit planning, market timing, and preparation of portfolio companies for exit scenarios are critical for managing exit risk.

In conclusion, while PE offers the potential for significant returns, it comes with a spectrum of risks that require diligent management. A deep understanding of these risks, coupled with strategic planning and active portfolio management, is crucial for investors and PE firms aiming to navigate the complexities of Private Equity successfully. By addressing these risks proactively, stakeholders can optimize their investment strategies and achieve their long-term objectives in the dynamic world of Private Equity.

New Trends in Private Equity

The Private Equity (PE) landscape is continually evolving, shaped by broader economic trends, technological advancements, and shifts in investor priorities. As we navigate through these changes, several key trends are emerging that promise to redefine the strategies and focus areas of PE firms in the coming years.

The Rise of Technology-Driven Investments

Technology has become a central theme in PE investments, with firms increasingly focusing on technology-driven companies and startups. This trend is driven by the recognition of technology's potential to disrupt traditional industries and create new markets. PE firms are investing in software, fintech, healthtech, and other tech-enabled sectors, aiming to capitalize on digital transformation opportunities.

Technology-Driven Value Creation
Levers and Tools for the hybrid work environment

Remote collaboration
- Optimizing workflow connectivity
  Real-time engagement through productivity platforms: Webex, Jabber, Slack and Symphony
- Global information ecosystem
  Dive, interactive town halls
  Lazard IQ knowledge center
  Tech academy training
- Business continuity planning
  - Critical function capabilities

Infrastructure & Analytics
- Virtual network access
  Secure remote-access
  Enhanced cyber-security
- High-power processing
  - Portfolio evaluation and execution, compliance and risk management
- Enterprise finance / risk
  - Centralized global platform

Customer-centric solutions
- Data privacy
  Multi-factor authentication
  Secure and single-source
- Transaction execution
  Data room due diligence
  Trade processing
- Digitization and personalization
  - 360 portfolio view
  - Specialized solutions

SAMPLE

CLOUD BASED DATA PLATFORM
Adopting Technology architecture built to support firm-wide data and analytics initiatives in a global and scalable enterprise model

Emphasis on Environmental, Social, and Governance (ESG) Criteria

ESG considerations have moved to the forefront of investment decisions, driven by growing awareness of climate change, social inequality, and corporate governance issues. PE firms are integrating ESG criteria into their investment processes, recognizing that sustainable and responsible investments can drive long-term value creation. This shift reflects a broader societal demand for more ethical and sustainable business practices.

Increased Focus on Operational Excellence

Operational excellence has become a critical differentiator for PE firms seeking to maximize the value of their portfolio companies. Beyond financial engineering, PE firms are placing greater emphasis on driving operational improvements, leveraging technology, and implementing best practices to enhance efficiency, innovation, and competitiveness.

Expansion into New Geographies

PE firms are expanding their geographic focus, seeking opportunities in emerging markets and regions with high growth potential. This trend is fueled by the search for untapped markets, diversification benefits, and the desire to capitalize on global economic shifts. However, this expansion requires careful consideration of geopolitical risks, regulatory environments, and cultural nuances.

Growing Popularity of Co-Investments

Co-investments, where investors directly invest alongside PE firms in specific deals, are gaining popularity. This trend allows investors to gain exposure to direct investments with lower fee structures while enabling PE firms to secure additional capital for larger deals. Co-investments offer mutual benefits, including enhanced returns and closer partnerships between PE firms and their investors.

The Advent of Secondary Markets for PE

The development of secondary markets for PE interests is providing liquidity solutions for investors. Secondary transactions, involving the sale of existing PE fund interests, are becoming more common, offering investors an avenue to exit their investments before the fund's maturity. This trend is contributing to the overall liquidity and flexibility of the PE asset class.

In conclusion, the PE industry is at a pivotal moment, with latest trends reshaping investment strategies and priorities. Technology-driven investments, ESG integration, operational excellence, geographic expansion, co-investments, and the development of secondary markets are among the key trends influencing the future of PE. As these trends continue to evolve, PE firms and investors alike must adapt and innovate to thrive in the dynamic landscape of Private Equity.

Global Private Equity AUM: A Titan's Grasp on Global Business

The global landscape of Private Equity (PE) is not just expansive; it is titanic, wielding a profound influence that reaches into the core of industries worldwide. With Assets Under Management (AUM) ballooning into the trillions, PE stands as a monumental force, one that commands control stakes in leading companies across the spectrum. This dominion places PE, alongside hedge funds, in a position where it can be argued they almost control the world's corporate sector.

The Magnitude of Influence

The magnitude of PE's influence is underscored by its vast AUM, reflecting a deep pool of capital ready to be deployed in acquiring, optimizing, and eventually divesting businesses for profit. This capital is not just idle; it is actively seeking and shaping the future of companies, industries, and, by extension, economies. With each investment, PE firms take on significant stakes, often gaining control over their portfolio companies, steering strategic directions, operational improvements, and long-term planning.

A Diverse Portfolio of Global Powerhouses

PE's portfolio is as diverse as it is extensive, encompassing everything from nascent tech startups to well-established multinational corporations. This diversity allows PE firms to spread their influence across various sectors, including technology, healthcare, consumer goods, financial services, and more. The breadth of their investments means that, in many ways, PE firms are behind some of the most significant innovations and strategic shifts in the market today.

The Strategy Behind the Control

The strategic acquisition of control stakes in leading companies is a deliberate one, allowing PE firms to implement transformative changes, drive efficiency, and accelerate growth. This level of influence is not just about financial returns; it is about reshaping industries, fostering innovation, and sometimes even setting the course for new market trends. The operational expertise and strategic guidance PE firms bring to their portfolio companies can be the catalyst for profound competitive advantage and market leadership.

The Global Reach

PE's global reach is unparalleled, with investments spanning every continent and market. This international presence not only diversifies the risk but also amplifies the impact PE firms have on the global business landscape. By moving capital across borders, PE firms facilitate the flow of innovation, best practices, and strategic alliances, further cementing their role as global economic architects.

A Responsibility to Steer Wisely

With great power comes great responsibility. The control that PE firms wield over the global corporate sector is a double-edged sword. While it enables rapid transformation and innovation, it also places a significant ethical and strategic burden on these firms to steer their portfolio companies wisely. The decisions made in boardrooms of PE-owned companies can have far-reaching implications for employees, consumers, and economies at large.

In conclusion, the global AUM of Private Equity is not just a number; it is a testament to the colossal role PE plays in shaping the corporate world. With control stakes in leading companies across various sectors, PE firms are at the forefront of steering strategic, operational, and even cultural shifts in the global business ecosystem. As the PE landscape continues to evolve, its influence on the global stage is set to grow even further, underlining the importance of responsible and visionary leadership within the PE community.

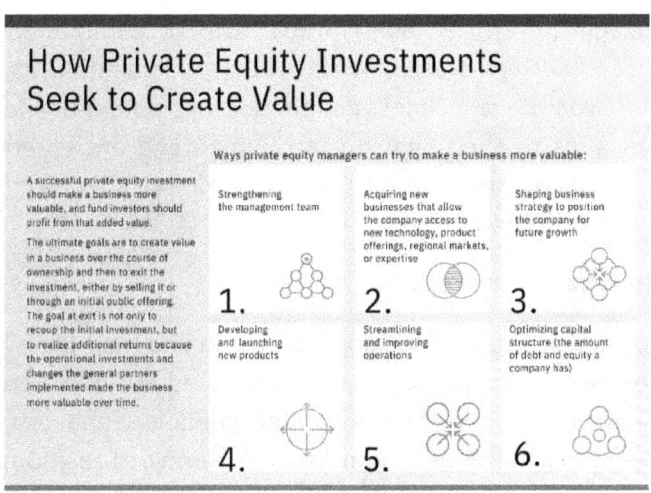

The PE Titan - $115 Trillion at 5% Growth Rate

The estimated global Assets Under Management (AUM) in Private Equity for 2023 experienced a decline to $115.1 trillion, 10% below the 2021 high of $127.5 trillion. This downturn marked the most significant decrease observed in a decade. However, forecasts suggest a rebound by 2027, with AUM projected to reach $147.3 trillion, indicating a compound annual growth rate (CAGR) of 5%.

Demystifying Private Equity: Beyond the Acronym

Private Equity (PE), often seen through a lens of complex financial strategies and high-stakes investments, fundamentally revolves around two core principles: people and entrepreneurship. This chapter aims to shed light on the human and entrepreneurial spirit that drives the PE industry, offering a fresh perspective on its mechanisms and impact.

The Essence of Private Equity

At its heart, PE is about investing in people and their ideas. It is a partnership where investors, often seasoned business veterans, back entrepreneurs with the capital, guidance, and resources they need to grow their businesses. This symbiotic relationship is built on a foundation of trust, mutual respect, and a shared vision for what a company can become.

The Role of Trust and Reputation

In PE, reputation is everything. Deals are made based not just on the numbers but on the confidence in an individual's or a team's ability to deliver on their promises. The industry operates on a network of relationships where a handshake can often carry as much weight as a signed contract. Trust, integrity, and a track record of success are the currencies of the realm.

Navigating the Landscape

For entrepreneurs, navigating the PE landscape can be daunting. It is a world where immense resources can be mobilized quickly, but where the expectations are sky-high. PE investors look for leaders who can not only envision a path to growth but who can also steer their companies through the challenges and opportunities that rapid scaling brings.

The Impact of PE Investments

The impact of PE goes beyond the financial returns. It is about building companies that last, that innovate, and that contribute to the economy in meaningful ways. From revitalizing struggling businesses to launching groundbreaking innovative technologies, PE plays a crucial role in the business ecosystem.

Challenges and Misconceptions

The PE industry is not without its challenges and controversies. Criticisms include its focus on short-term gains, aggressive cost-cutting measures, and a lack of transparency. However, many PE firms are evolving, adopting more sustainable investment strategies, and focusing on long-term value creation for all stakeholders.

A Path Forward

Looking ahead, the PE industry continues to adapt and innovate. There is a growing emphasis on environmental, social, and governance (ESG) factors, reflecting a broader shift towards responsible investment practices. As PE firms embrace these changes, they not only enhance their own reputations but also contribute to a more sustainable and equitable global economy.

In conclusion, Private Equity is more than just a financial mechanism; it is a dynamic force that shapes industries and transforms businesses. By focusing on the people and the entrepreneurial ventures they embark on, PE plays a pivotal role in driving progress and innovation in the global marketplace.

Part 2: Private Equity - The Players

Who are the players?

The Deal Teams
The Operating Partners

The PE Players: Deal Teams and Operational Value Creation Teams

In the dynamic world of Private Equity (PE), success hinges not only on identifying lucrative investment opportunities but also on enhancing the value of portfolio companies post-acquisition. This dual focus is navigated by two critical cohorts within PE firms: Deal Teams and Operational Value Creation (OVC) Teams. Each plays a distinct yet interconnected role in driving the PE investment lifecycle towards its goal: maximizing returns.

Deal Teams are the scouts and strategists of the PE world. Their primary mission is to identify, assess, and secure investment opportunities that align with the firm's strategic objectives. This involves meticulous market research, financial analysis, and negotiation to structure deals that promise substantial returns. Deal Teams are often seen as the architects of a PE firm's portfolio, laying the groundwork for future value creation through their keen sense of market dynamics and investment opportunities.

Operational Value Creation (OVC) Teams, on the other hand, are the artisans of post-acquisition value enhancement. Once a deal is sealed, the baton is passed to OVC Teams who work closely with portfolio companies to drive operational improvements, strategic pivots, and growth initiatives. Their expertise spans various domains, including finance, operations, marketing, and human resources, allowing them to implement bespoke solutions tailored to each company's unique challenges and opportunities. OVC Teams embody the principle that while acquiring a company is a matter of financial investment, transforming it requires a deep dive into its operational fabric.

Together, Deal Teams and OVC Teams form the backbone of a PE firm's ability to not just invest but to transform. While Deal Teams navigate the complexities of the market to secure valuable assets, OVC Teams ensure those assets are polished to shine their brightest. This symbiotic relationship between scouting for potential and realizing that potential is what sets PE apart as not just a financial endeavor, but a transformative force in the business world.

In the chapters that follow, we will delve deeper into the mechanisms of Operational Value Creation, outlining the strategies, challenges, and successes that define this essential aspect of Private Equity.

Part 2a: The Players – The PE Deal Teams

The Role of Deal Teams in PE

In the dynamic ecosystem of Private Equity (PE), Deal Teams emerge as pivotal players, orchestrating the complex symphony of identifying, securing, and nurturing investment opportunities. These teams serve as the vanguard of PE firms, meticulously evaluating and executing deals that align with strategic objectives, thereby ensuring the sustained growth and profitability of portfolio companies. The essence of their role transcends mere transactional activities, embedding them deeply within the fabric of value creation and operational excellence.

The Symbiosis with Operational Partners (OP)

Deal Teams and Operational Value Creation (OVC) initiatives, along with Operational Partners (OPs), form a strategic triad within the PE framework. This collaboration is instrumental in sculpting the trajectory of portfolio companies towards their zenith of performance and market competitiveness. Deal Teams lay the groundwork through diligent deal sourcing and execution, setting the stage for OVC strategies to be implemented. OPs, with their nuanced understanding of industry trends and operational intricacies, then step in to drive transformative changes within these companies. This synergistic approach ensures that investments are not only sound from a financial standpoint but are also ripe for operational enhancements that spur long-term growth.

Strategic Significance in Deal Sourcing

The inception of any successful PE investment begins with the adeptness of Deal Teams in sourcing lucrative opportunities. Their strategic acumen in identifying potential investments that align with the firm's vision and objectives is paramount. Through a combination of industry insight, network leverage, and analytical prowess, Deal Teams navigate the vast landscape of possibilities to unearth gems that promise high returns. This phase is critical, as it lays the foundation for the subsequent stages of value creation and growth.

Meticulous Execution and Portfolio Integration

Post identification, the baton passes to the meticulous process of deal execution. Here, the Deal Teams' expertise is put to the test as they navigate negotiations, due diligence, and the complexities of closing transactions. The goal is not only to seal the deal but to do so in a manner that positions the portfolio company for seamless integration and alignment with the PE firm's strategic goals. This phase demands a deep understanding of legal frameworks, financial structuring, and strategic foresight to anticipate and mitigate potential challenges that could impede the integration process.

Ongoing Portfolio Management

With the deal securely under the PE firm's umbrella, Deal Teams continue to play a crucial role in portfolio management. This involves continuous monitoring and strategic decision-making to ensure the portfolio company not only meets but exceeds expected performance metrics. Deal Teams work in close concert with OPs to identify areas for operational improvements, market expansion, and potential exits that maximize returns. This ongoing engagement ensures that the portfolio company remains on a trajectory of growth and profitability, reflecting the strategic value of the initial investment.

The role of Deal Teams within the PE landscape is multifaceted and integral to the success of investment endeavors. From the initial stages of deal sourcing to the ongoing management of portfolio companies, their strategic insights and execution capabilities are indispensable. In collaboration with OPs and underpinned by OVC initiatives, Deal Teams ensure that investments are not just financially sound but are also primed for operational excellence and strategic growth. As the PE industry continues to evolve, the importance of Deal Teams in navigating this complex and competitive landscape only becomes more pronounced, highlighting their indispensable role in driving the future success of PE investments.

Anatomy of a PE Deal

The anatomy of a Private Equity (PE) Deal Team is as complex as it is critical to the successful execution of investments. At its core, a PE Deal Team consists of a group of professionals with a diverse set of skills and expertise, united by a common goal: to identify, evaluate, execute, and manage investments that will yield high returns. This composition is not static; it evolves based on the deal's requirements, the stage of investment, and the specific needs of the portfolio company.

The Anatomy of a Private Equity Deal Team

Managing Partner	Investment Director
Vision and fundraising	Deal execution

Operating Partner	Risk Analyst
Portfolio value creation	Due diligence and risk mitigation

Team Definition and Composition A typical PE Deal Team includes a mix of senior and junior members, each bringing their own unique perspectives and expertise to the table. The team is often led by a Deal Lead or Partner, who is responsible for overseeing the investment process from start to finish. Supporting the Deal Lead are Associates and Analysts, who handle much of the research, due diligence, and financial modeling. In more complex transactions, the team may also include specialists in areas such as legal, tax, and operational improvement.

Roles and Responsibilities within the Deal Team The Deal Lead is the architect of the investment, setting the strategy, making critical decisions, and leading negotiations with sellers and other stakeholders. They are responsible for the ultimate success or failure of the investment and, as such, must have a deep understanding of the industry, market trends, and investment opportunities.

Associates and Analysts are the workhorses of the Deal Team, conducting detailed industry research, financial analysis, and due diligence to identify and evaluate potential investment opportunities. They prepare investment memorandums and presentations for the investment committee and may also be involved in the post-acquisition integration and management of the portfolio company.

Specialists such as legal and tax advisors provide critical support in their areas of expertise, ensuring that all aspects of the deal are thoroughly vetted and compliant with relevant regulations and best practices.

Skills and Expertise Required for Effective Deal Execution Successful deal execution requires a blend of technical skills, industry knowledge, and soft skills. Technical skills include financial modeling, valuation, and due diligence, which are foundational to evaluating and executing investments. Industry knowledge is critical for understanding the competitive landscape, trends, and growth drivers that will affect the investment's success.

Soft skills are equally important, as Deal Team members must be able to negotiate effectively, build relationships with stakeholders, and manage the complexities of the investment process. Leadership and teamwork are crucial, as the Deal Team must work cohesively to navigate the challenges and opportunities that arise during the investment lifecycle.

Effective communication is another key skill, as Deal Team members must articulate their findings, strategies, and recommendations to the investment committee, portfolio company management, and other stakeholders.

Conclusion The anatomy of a PE Deal Team reflects the multifaceted nature of private equity investing. The composition of the team, roles, and responsibilities, and required skills and expertise are all tailored to the unique challenges and opportunities of each investment. By combining technical prowess with industry insight and strong leadership and communication skills, PE Deal Teams are equipped to execute successful investments that drive value for their firms and stakeholders. This intricate blend of talent and expertise underscores the critical role of the Deal Team in the PE investment process, from initial sourcing to final exit.

A High-Pressure Play

Deal Teams in Private Equity (PE) are notably financed by the management fees collected by the PE firm from its investors, typically ranging from 2% to 2.5% of the fund's total assets under management (AUM). This financial structure means that for a fund worth $500 million, for instance, there is approximately $10 million to $12.5 million available annually to support the firm's operations, including compensating its Deal Team. This financial model underscores the necessity for each member of the Deal Team to pull their weight, both literally and metaphorically. The limited pool of funds allocated for staffing highlights the premium placed on efficiency, expertise, and the ability to contribute significantly to the fund's success. Therefore, in the high-stakes environment of PE, every team member's contribution is crucial, with the expectation that their work directly influences the fund's overall performance and, by extension, its ability to deliver superior returns to its investors. This economic dynamic fosters a culture of high performance and accountability within PE Deal Teams, as the financial viability of the team itself hinges on the successful execution and management of investments that drive value creation.

Deal Sourcing and Evaluation Strategies

Deal Sourcing and Evaluation Strategies in Private Equity (PE) Deal Teams play a critical role in identifying and assessing potential investment opportunities, a process that is both art and science. This chapter delves into the methodologies employed by Deal Teams for deal sourcing and the meticulous evaluation strategies that underpin successful investments. It also presents real-world case studies to illustrate these practices in action.

Deal Sourcing: The Hunt for Opportunities

Deal sourcing in PE involves a proactive search for potential investment targets that meet specific criteria set by the PE firm. This process is highly strategic and often relies on a mix of industry knowledge, network connections, and market analysis. Deal Teams leverage various channels for deal sourcing, including:

- **Direct Outreach:** Approaching potential targets directly, often businesses not actively looking to sell but that fit the PE firm's investment thesis.

- **Intermediaries:** Utilizing investment bankers, brokers, and advisors who provide access to deals and can facilitate introductions.

- **Industry Events and Conferences:** Networking at events relevant to the PE firm's focus areas to uncover opportunities and foster relationships.

- **Proprietary Deals:** Cultivating exclusive opportunities through relationships and reputation, avoiding competitive bidding processes.

Initial Evaluation and Due Diligence

Once a potential deal is identified, the Deal Team undertakes an initial evaluation to determine its suitability and potential for value creation. This phase includes:

- **Preliminary Screening:** Assessing the company against the PE firm's investment criteria, such as industry, size, growth potential, and strategic fit.
- **Financial Analysis:** Reviewing financial statements, performance metrics, and forecasts to understand the company's financial health and prospects.
- **Market Assessment:** Evaluating the target's market position, competitive landscape, and growth opportunities.
- **Management Interviews:** Meeting with the company's leadership to gauge their vision, capability, and alignment with the PE firm's objectives.

Following the initial evaluation, the Deal Team conducts comprehensive due diligence, a deep dive into the company's operations, financials, legal matters, and market position to identify any risks or issues that could affect the investment's success.

Case Studies: Success in the Field

Several case studies exemplify the effectiveness of robust deal sourcing and evaluation strategies:

1. **Tech Buyout:** A PE firm identified a niche software company through direct outreach, recognizing its potential to disrupt a larger market. Initial evaluations revealed a strong management team and scalable product. Comprehensive due diligence confirmed the

company's growth trajectory, leading to a successful acquisition and subsequent value creation through market expansion and operational improvements.

2. **Healthcare Sector Deal:** Leveraging an intermediary, a Deal Team discovered a healthcare services company poised for growth but needing capital and strategic guidance. Preliminary screening and due diligence highlighted the opportunity for operational efficiencies and expansion into new markets. The investment proved extraordinarily successful, with significant returns generated through strategic initiatives and eventual sale to a larger industry player.

3. **Manufacturing Industry Turnaround:** At an industry conference, a Deal Team initiated discussions with a family-owned manufacturing business facing succession challenges. The evaluation process uncovered undervalued assets and opportunities for modernization and efficiency improvements. Post-acquisition, the PE firm implemented operational enhancements and strategic acquisitions, dramatically increasing the company's value.

These case studies demonstrate the critical importance of effective deal sourcing and evaluation strategies, underscoring the Deal Team's role in driving successful PE investments. Through meticulous processes and strategic insights, Deal Teams can uncover and capitalize on opportunities that offer substantial returns, reinforcing the value of Private Equity as a transformative force in the business landscape.

Deal Execution and Portfolio Integration

Deal execution and portfolio integration are pivotal stages in the private equity (PE) investment cycle, where strategic planning transitions into actionable steps to secure and optimize new assets. This chapter explores the multifaceted process of executing deals and the subsequent integration of portfolio companies, highlighting strategies, challenges, and best practices.

Deal Execution: From Negotiation to Closing

Deal execution encompasses all activities from the initial agreement to the final acquisition of a target company. It is a phase characterized by meticulous negotiation, thorough due diligence, and the coordination of legal and financial frameworks. Key steps include:

- **Finalizing the Deal Structure:** PE Deal Teams work closely with legal advisors to determine the most advantageous deal structure, considering tax implications, financing arrangements, and regulatory compliance.

- **Negotiation:** This involves discussions on price, terms, and conditions with the target company's stakeholders. Successful negotiation requires a deep understanding of the target's value proposition and strategic leverage.

- **Due Diligence:** Beyond the initial evaluation, this in-depth review covers financial, legal, operational, and compliance aspects to uncover any potential risks or liabilities.

- **Financing:** Securing the necessary funding for the acquisition, which may involve a mix of equity, debt, and sometimes, creative financing solutions like earn-outs or seller financing.

- **Closing:** The culmination of the execution phase, where legal documents are signed, funds are transferred, and control of the target company is officially transferred to the PE firm.

Portfolio Integration: Aligning with PE Firm Objectives

Once a deal is closed, the focus shifts to integrating the new portfolio company and aligning it with the PE firm's strategic objectives. Effective integration is critical for realizing the value creation plan and involves:

- **Strategic Planning:** Developing a 100-day plan to prioritize initiatives that drive immediate value, such as operational improvements, cost reductions, and revenue growth strategies.

- **Cultural Integration:** Bridging cultural differences between the PE firm and the portfolio company, fostering a shared vision, and ensuring buy-in from key stakeholders.

- **Operational Optimization:** Implementing best practices in operations, finance, HR, and IT to enhance efficiency and performance.

- **Governance and Leadership:** Establishing a governance structure that supports accountability and aligning leadership roles with the company's strategic direction.

Challenges and Best Practices

Deal execution and portfolio integration present several challenges, from unexpected due diligence findings to resistance from the portfolio company's existing management. Best practices for overcoming these challenges include:

- **Effective Communication:** Maintaining open lines of communication with all stakeholders throughout the deal execution and integration process to manage expectations and address concerns.
- **Flexibility:** Being prepared to adapt strategies in response to latest information or changing market conditions.
- **Experienced Advisors:** Leveraging the expertise of legal, financial, and industry advisors to navigate complex deal structures and integration hurdles.
- **Employee Engagement:** Actively engaging the portfolio company's employees to ensure a smooth transition and minimize disruption.

Real-World Example

A notable example of successful deal execution and portfolio integration involved a mid-sized PE firm acquiring a regional logistics company. Through careful negotiation, the PE firm secured favorable terms that allowed for significant investment in technology upgrades. The integration process focused on operational efficiencies, leading to improved route optimization and cost savings. Strategic leadership changes and a redefined company culture resulted in increased employee engagement and customer satisfaction, driving substantial growth in revenue and profitability.

In conclusion, deal execution and portfolio integration are critical for the success of PE investments. By adhering to best practices and overcoming the inherent challenges, PE firms can effectively integrate new portfolio companies, aligning them with strategic objectives and setting the stage for significant value creation.

Portfolio Management and Value Maximization

The essence of Private Equity (PE) lies not just in the adept execution of deals but also in the nuanced art of portfolio management and value maximization. This chapter delves into the integral role of Deal Teams in the ongoing stewardship of portfolio companies, detailing their collaborative efforts with Operational Partners (OPs) to foster growth and enhance value. It also outlines the metrics and Key Performance Indicators (KPIs) pivotal for monitoring performance and guiding strategic decisions.

The Role of Deal Teams in Portfolio Management

Deal Teams extend their involvement beyond the acquisition phase, playing a crucial role in the strategic oversight and management of portfolio companies. This ongoing engagement is critical for ensuring that each portfolio company aligns with the PE firm's overarching investment thesis and objectives. Deal Teams are instrumental in:

- **Strategic Planning:** Setting clear, long-term strategic goals for each portfolio company, including market expansion, product development, and operational efficiency improvements.

- **Financial Oversight:** Monitoring financial performance against projections and industry benchmarks to ensure financial health and identify areas for improvement.

- **Governance:** Participating in or directly influencing the governance structures of portfolio companies, often through board representation, to ensure strategic alignment and accountability.

Collaborating with Operational Partners for Value Creation

The symbiosis between Deal Teams and Operational Partners (OPs) is a cornerstone of effective portfolio management. While Deal Teams provide strategic and financial oversight, OPs bring deep operational expertise to drive tangible improvements. This collaboration is manifested through:

- **Joint Value Creation Plans:** Developing and implementing detailed value creation plans that leverage both the strategic insights of Deal Teams and the operational acumen of OPs.

- **Regular Performance Reviews:** Conducting periodic reviews of operational and financial performance to assess progress against value creation targets and adjust strategies as needed.

- **Cross-portfolio Initiatives:** Identifying and implementing best practices and learnings across the portfolio to drive efficiency and innovation.

Metrics and KPIs for Portfolio Performance Assessment

Deal Teams rely on a comprehensive set of metrics and KPIs to assess the performance of portfolio companies and make informed strategic decisions. Key metrics include:

- **Financial Performance Indicators:** Revenue growth, EBITDA margins, cash flow generation, and return on invested capital (ROIC) are critical for assessing the financial health and operational efficiency of portfolio companies.

- **Operational Metrics:** Customer satisfaction scores, employee engagement levels, production efficiency, and supply chain reliability offer insights into the operational strengths and weaknesses of portfolio companies.

- **Strategic Milestones:** Progress against strategic initiatives, such as market entry, product launches, and M&A activity, helps gauge the success of long-term growth strategies.

Real-World Example

A notable instance of effective portfolio management involved a PE firm that acquired a consumer goods company. The Deal Team, in collaboration with OPs, identified key areas for operational improvements, including supply chain optimization and digital marketing initiatives. Through rigorous performance monitoring and strategic guidance, the company achieved significant improvements in operational efficiency and market share growth, culminating in a successful exit at a multiple of the initial investment.

In conclusion, Deal Teams play a vital role in the ongoing management and value maximization of portfolio companies. Through strategic collaboration with OPs and the judicious use of metrics and KPIs, they ensure that portfolio companies not only meet but exceed their performance targets. This holistic approach to portfolio management underpins the PE firm's ability to deliver superior returns to its investors, cementing its reputation in the competitive landscape of private equity.

The Evolving Role of Deal Teams in PE

In the ever-dynamic world of Private Equity (PE), the role of Deal Teams is continuously adapting to the seismic shifts and innovations reshaping the investment landscape. This chapter explores the emerging trends and technological advancements influencing the methodologies and operations of Deal Teams. It highlights how these changes are necessitating strategic recalibrations within PE firms to empower Deal Teams, ensuring they remain agile and effective in a rapidly evolving market.

Emerging Trends Influencing Deal Teams

Several key trends are transforming the landscape of PE, each posing unique challenges and opportunities for Deal Teams:

- **Increased Competition for Deals:** With more capital chasing fewer deals, Deal Teams are under pressure to identify and secure investment opportunities faster than ever. This competitive environment is driving the adoption of advanced data analytics and AI to enhance deal sourcing and evaluation processes.

- **Focus on ESG and Impact Investing:** Environmental, Social, and Governance (ESG) factors and impact investing are becoming critical considerations in the investment decision-making process. Deal Teams are now tasked with integrating ESG assessments into their due diligence and valuation models, ensuring alignment with evolving investor priorities and regulatory landscapes.

- **Technological Disruption:** Rapid technological advancements across industries are forcing Deal Teams to become adept at evaluating tech-driven business models and digital transformation opportunities within potential and existing portfolio companies.

The Impact of Technological Advancements on Deal Team Methodologies

Technological innovations are profoundly affecting how Deal Teams operate, offering new tools and approaches for enhancing efficiency and accuracy:

- **Big Data and Predictive Analytics:** The use of big data and predictive analytics is enabling Deal Teams to uncover insights and identify investment opportunities with a level of precision previously unattainable. These technologies facilitate the analysis of market trends, competitive landscapes, and potential target performance in real-time.

- **Blockchain and Smart Contracts:** Blockchain technology and smart contracts are streamlining transaction processes, reducing the time and cost associated with deal execution. They also offer enhanced security and transparency in investment transactions.

- **AI and Machine Learning:** AI and machine learning tools are revolutionizing deal sourcing and due diligence by automating the analysis of vast amounts of data, identifying patterns, and predicting outcomes with high accuracy.

Strategic Considerations for PE Firms

To remain competitive and maximize the effectiveness of their Deal Teams, PE firms must consider several strategic actions:

- **Investing in Training and Development:** PE firms should invest in continuous training and development programs to equip Deal Teams with the skills needed to navigate modern technologies and methodologies.

- **Fostering a Culture of Innovation:** Encouraging a culture of innovation within Deal Teams can drive the adoption of new tools and approaches, ensuring the firm stays at the forefront of industry advancements.

- **Collaboration Across Functions:** Enhancing collaboration between Deal Teams, Operational Partners, and technology specialists can foster a more integrated approach to deal sourcing, evaluation, and value creation.

The role of Deal Teams within the PE industry is evolving in response to technological advancements, market shifts, and changing investor expectations. By embracing emerging trends, investing in innovative technologies, and fostering a culture of continuous learning and innovation, PE firms can empower their Deal Teams to navigate the complexities of the modern investment landscape effectively. This forward-thinking approach will not only enhance the efficiency and effectiveness of Deal Teams but also position PE firms to capitalize on new opportunities and drive superior returns in an increasingly competitive market.

Part 2b: The Players - OVC and Operational Partners

The Essence of Operational Value Creation in PE

Operational Value Creation (OVC) has become a cornerstone in the realm of Private Equity (PE), distinguishing itself as a vital strategy beyond traditional financial engineering. At its core, OVC embodies the deliberate efforts to enhance the operational efficiency, innovation, and growth potential of portfolio companies. This strategic approach allows PE firms to unlock value from within, driving sustainable improvements that contribute to the overall success and competitiveness of their investments.

Why OVC Matters in Private Equity

OVC stands out for several reasons in the PE ecosystem:

- **Beyond Financial Engineering:** In the early days of PE, firms primarily relied on financial restructuring to realize gains. However, as markets evolved and competition intensified, the focus shifted towards generating operational improvements as a more sustainable source of value.

- **Adaptability and Resilience:** The dynamic nature of today's business environment demands adaptability. OVC equips portfolio companies with the agility needed to navigate market changes, regulatory shifts, and technological advancements, ensuring long-term resilience.

- **Competitive Differentiation:** By implementing OVC strategies, PE firms can differentiate their portfolio companies in crowded markets. Operational improvements, whether through cost reduction, revenue enhancement, or innovation, can provide a competitive edge that attracts customers, talent, and further investment.

The Role of Operational Partners (OPs)

Operational Partners play a pivotal role in executing OVC strategies. These individuals or teams bring deep industry expertise, operational experience, and a hands-on approach to driving change within portfolio companies. They work closely with management teams to identify opportunities for improvement, implement best practices, and oversee the execution of strategic initiatives.

Key Objectives of OVC

The primary objectives of OVC in PE include:

- **Enhancing Operational Efficiency:** Streamlining processes, optimizing resource allocation, and improving supply chain management to reduce costs and increase profitability.

- **Driving Revenue Growth:** Identifying new market opportunities, enhancing product offerings, and improving sales and marketing effectiveness to drive top-line growth.

- **Fostering Innovation:** Encouraging the development of new products, services, and business models to keep pace with market trends and customer demands.

The Impact of OVC

The impact of OVC on portfolio companies and their stakeholders can be profound. Operational improvements not only enhance financial performance but also strengthen the company's market position, employee satisfaction, and customer loyalty. Moreover, successful OVC initiatives can significantly increase the attractiveness of a company to potential buyers or public market investors, leading to higher exit valuations for PE firms.

In conclusion, Operational Value Creation is a critical element in the value proposition of Private Equity, offering a path to sustainable growth and competitive advantage. As the PE industry continues to evolve, the emphasis on OVC is likely to increase, underscoring the importance of Operational Partners and innovative strategies in driving the success of PE investments.

Operational Partners: The Architects of Value

In the realm of Private Equity (PE), Operational Partners (OPs) stand as pivotal figures, orchestrating substantial transformations within portfolio companies. These professionals are not merely advisors but are actively involved in steering these companies towards achieving their strategic objectives. This chapter delves into the essence, roles, and remarkable impacts of OPs, drawing from their vast reservoirs of expertise to unlock unparalleled value.

Defining the Role and Responsibilities

Operational Partners are seasoned experts, often with extensive executive or industry-specific experience, tasked with driving operational improvements and strategic initiatives. Unlike traditional consultants, OPs work closely with the management teams of portfolio companies, providing hands-on guidance and support to implement best practices, enhance operational efficiencies, and foster growth. Their responsibilities may span various domains, including finance, marketing, IT, and human resources, tailored to address the specific needs and challenges of each portfolio company.

The Skill Sets and Expertise Required

The effectiveness of an Operational Partner hinges on a diverse skill set that blends strategic vision with operational acumen. Key competencies include:

- **Strategic Planning**: The ability to develop and execute robust business strategies that align with the company's long-term objectives.

- **Operational Excellence**: Expertise in optimizing business processes, improving supply chain management, and enhancing productivity.

- **Leadership and Change Management**: Strong leadership qualities to drive organizational change, inspire teams, and cultivate a culture of continuous improvement.

- **Financial Acumen**: A deep understanding of fiscal management, enabling OPs to identify cost-saving opportunities and drive profitability.

Case Studies: Transformative Impact

Illustrative case studies underscore the transformative role of Operational Partners in reshaping portfolio companies:

1. **Turnaround Success**: A manufacturing firm, grappling with operational inefficiencies and stagnant growth, partners with a PE firm. The assigned Operational Partner overhauls the production processes, reducing waste and downtime, leading to a remarkable turnaround in profitability and market competitiveness.

2. **Growth Acceleration**: An e-commerce startup, struggling to scale, benefits from the expertise of an Operational Partner who streamlines its logistics and customer service operations. The result is an exponential increase in customer satisfaction and sales, propelling the company into a phase of rapid expansion.

Challenges and Best Practices

While the integration of Operational Partners can catalyze significant value creation, it is not devoid of challenges. Ensuring alignment with the company's culture, managing stakeholder expectations, and navigating resistance to change are common hurdles. Best practices for overcoming these challenges include establishing clear communication channels, setting measurable goals, and fostering a collaborative environment that encourages innovation and risk-taking.

Operational Partners are indispensable assets in the PE ecosystem, their contributions far surpassing mere advisory roles. By embedding themselves within portfolio companies, they unlock potential, drive innovation, and significantly impact the bottom line. As the PE landscape continues to evolve, the role of OPs will undoubtedly become more critical, underscoring their status as true architects of value in the dynamic world of Private Equity.

OVC Strategies and Implementation

Operational Value Creation (OVC) Strategies and Implementation in Private Equity involve a multifaceted approach to enhancing the value of portfolio companies beyond financial structuring. By focusing on operational improvements, PE firms can significantly impact the performance and growth of their investments. Here is an overview based on the provided content and general practices in the industry:

Value Creation Levers: Professionalization and Scaling

Organizational Structure	Strategic Planning	Leadership Development	Financial Management
Private equity firms often implement efficient organizational structures, streamline reporting lines, and establish clear roles and responsibilities, enabling effective decision-making and faster execution.	Developing a comprehensive strategic plan, aligned with industry trends and market opportunities, is essential for sustainable growth.	Investing in leadership development programs can enhance the skills and capabilities of key executives, fostering a strong leadership team capable of navigating challenges and driving company performance.	Investors usually bring expertise in financial management, improving budgeting, forecasting and capital allocation. They can also guide companies in implementing strong financial controls and reporting mechanisms.

OVC Strategies Employed by PE Firms

1. **Operational Efficiency and Value Creation**: OPs are instrumental in driving operational efficiency, identifying areas for cost reduction, revenue growth, and overall performance enhancement.

2. **Risk Mitigation and Problem Solving**: Through proactive problem-solving, OPs help portfolio companies navigate challenges and mitigate risks, adding intrinsic value.

3. **Strategic Guidance and Decision-Making**: OPs contribute strategic insights, aiding in critical decision-making processes with their industry knowledge and operational expertise.

The Process of Implementing OVC Initiatives

- **Diagnostic Phase**: Identifying underlying issues and areas of opportunity within portfolio companies.

- **Strategy Formulation**: Developing comprehensive turnaround plans and operational improvements strategies.

- **Hands-On Execution**: Active participation in the implementation of strategies to drive change.

Challenges in OVC Execution

- **Aligning Stakeholder Expectations**: Ensuring transparent communication and aligning the strategic narrative with stakeholder expectations.

- **Resource Optimization**: Navigating the allocation of resources to high-impact areas during turnaround scenarios.

- **Sustainability**: Ensuring that operational improvements are sustainable and ingrained in the company's culture for long-term success.

Best Practices in OVC Execution

- **Balancing Cost and Value**: Evaluating the efficiency of OP engagements by considering the cost-to-value ratio and ensuring a strong alignment of interests through incentives.

- **Flexibility in Approach**: Tailoring OVC strategies based on the specific needs of each deal and the overall strategy of the PE firm.

- **Leveraging Technology**: Incorporating data analytics, AI, and automation tools to enhance operational efficiency and scalability.

Operational Value Creation in Private Equity is a dynamic and essential aspect of achieving long-term, sustainable growth in portfolio companies. By leveraging the expertise of Operational Partners and employing strategic OVC initiatives, PE firms can drive significant improvements in performance, navigate market and operational risks effectively, and generate substantial value for their investments. The implementation of these strategies requires careful planning, expertise, and a collaborative effort between the PE firm, its Operational Partners, and portfolio company management to ensure success.

Measuring the Impact of OVC and OP Engagement

Chapter 4 of the book focuses on measuring the impact of Operational Value Creation (OVC) and Operational Partner (OP) engagement within the private equity (PE) industry. This chapter delves into the intricacies of evaluating the effectiveness of OVC initiatives and the benefits brought about by the involvement of OPs. By employing a mix of quantitative and qualitative metrics, it sheds light on the real-world implications of these strategies, offering a comprehensive overview of their ROI.

Operational Value Creation (OVC) Teams and Operational Partners (OPs) are integral to the strategic enhancement of portfolio companies in the private equity (PE) sector. Their contributions, aimed at fostering growth, improving efficiency, and driving profitability, necessitate a robust framework for assessment. This chapter explores the key metrics and Key Performance Indicators (KPIs) utilized to gauge OVC effectiveness, underscores the quantitative and qualitative benefits of OP involvement, and presents real-world examples that illustrate the tangible ROI of these initiatives.

Metrics and KPIs for Assessing OVC Effectiveness

The evaluation of OVC initiatives hinges on a carefully curated set of metrics and KPIs designed to capture the nuances of operational improvements and strategic shifts. These metrics often encompass financial performance indicators such as EBITDA growth, revenue enhancement, cost reduction percentages, and capital expenditure efficiencies. Additionally, operational metrics like production turnaround times, customer satisfaction scores, and employee engagement levels provide a multi-dimensional view of OVC's impact.

Quantitative and Qualitative Benefits of OP Involvement

The involvement of Operational Partners (OPs) in PE investments yields both measurable and intangible benefits. Quantitatively, OPs contribute to the acceleration of revenue growth, the optimization of cost structures, and the realization of synergies post-acquisition. Qualitatively, their expertise enhances organizational capabilities, fosters innovation, and strengthens leadership and governance structures within portfolio companies. This dual impact underscores the multifaceted value OPs bring to the PE investment lifecycle.

Real-world Examples Demonstrating the ROI of OVC and OP Initiatives

Illustrative case studies of portfolio companies that have undergone transformative changes under the guidance of OVC strategies and OP stewardship further validate the effectiveness of these approaches. For instance, a technology firm struggling with stagnant growth and operational inefficiencies experienced a remarkable turnaround through strategic operational interventions, resulting in a significant uplift in its market valuation. Another example includes a manufacturing company that leveraged OVC to streamline its supply chain and optimize production processes, achieving double-digit growth in operational efficiency and profitability.

The strategic deployment of OVC and the engagement of OPs within the PE industry play a pivotal role in unlocking the potential of portfolio companies. By leveraging a comprehensive set of metrics and KPIs, PE firms can effectively measure the impact of these initiatives, ensuring that their investments are aligned with the objectives of sustainable growth and value creation. The real-world examples highlighted in this chapter serve as a testament to the transformative power of OVC and OP engagement, offering valuable insights and best practices for PE firms aiming to maximize their ROI.

The BHAG Approach

"...River Deep, Mountain High..."

People with great goals are like majestic lions with manes, boldly standing out to both shock and inspire. Now, imagine yourself flaunting the most fabulous afro hairdo on a grand stage— radiating utmost confidence and singing your heart out. It does not matter if you might encounter stumbles, or face slips, but rest assured, you will not merely be noticed; you will be engraved into memory. I say embrace the spirit of a Tina Turner – hustle, shine, whether in victory or defeat, for in the end, amidst the applause or the silence, they will always remember you... for your performance BHAGed them all!

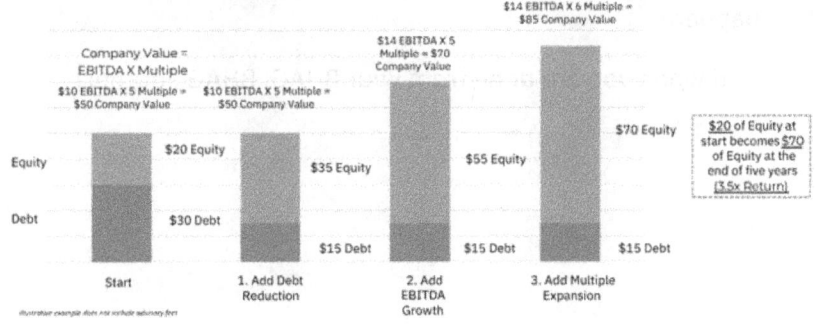

A BHAG, which stands for Big Hairy Audacious Goal, is like the superhero of business goals. It is the goals set by business leaders, CEOs, or Operating Partners to create maximum value. Picture it as this grand, audacious mission that is so big and hairy that it is like trying to tame a lion. You know, not your everyday kind of goal; it is the stuff legends are made of.

Now, why is it so cool? Well, a BHAG is like the company's GPS, but instead of just giving directions, it is pointing towards the Everest of achievements. It is not your typical goal you hit and forget; it is the kind that transforms the whole vibe of the workplace. Think of it as a massive shot of inspiration that makes everyone jump out of bed, excited to conquer the day.

So, this big, audacious thing is not just about hitting a target; it is about creating a buzz, sparking innovation, and turning a regular Tuesday into an epic quest. It is like telling your team, "Hey, we're not just here to play, we're here to change the game!" BHAGs make you dream big, push boundaries, and turn your company into a legend. It is not just a goal; it is an adventure waiting to happen!

And when you are done from your BHAG, BHAG another!

The Future of OVC and OP in Private Equity

This chapter delves into the future landscape of Operational Value Creation (OVC) and the role of Operational Partners (OPs) within the private equity (PE) industry. This chapter explores the emerging trends and innovations shaping OVC, examines the evolving PE landscape and its implications for OVC and OP strategies, and outlines strategic considerations for PE firms aiming to maximize the potential of their OVC and OP initiatives.

The Future of OVC and OP in Private Equity

The PE industry stands on the cusp of transformative changes, driven by advancements in technology, shifts in global economic dynamics, and evolving business models. These changes herald new opportunities and challenges for OVC and OPs, prompting a re-evaluation of traditional strategies and the exploration of innovative approaches to value creation.

Emerging Trends and Innovations in OVC and OP Roles

Emerging trends in technology, such as artificial intelligence (AI), machine learning, and big data analytics, are revolutionizing OVC practices. These technologies enable more sophisticated analysis of operational efficiencies, predictive modeling for business outcomes, and enhanced decision-making processes. Furthermore, the increasing focus on sustainability and ESG (Environmental, Social, and Governance) factors is shaping OVC strategies, with OPs playing a crucial role in integrating sustainable practices and governance models into portfolio companies.

The Evolving Landscape of the PE Industry and Implications for OVC/OP

The PE industry is experiencing shifts in investment patterns, with an increased emphasis on sector-specific funds, longer investment horizons, and the rise of impact investing. This evolving landscape necessitates adaptive OVC strategies and versatile OP roles, capable of navigating sector-specific challenges, driving long-term value creation, and aligning investments with broader societal and environmental objectives.

Strategic Considerations for PE Firms to Maximize OVC and OP Potential

To harness the full potential of OVC and OPs in the changing PE environment, firms must adopt a strategic and forward-looking approach. This involves investing in talent and technology that can drive innovation in OVC practices, fostering a culture of continuous learning and adaptability among OPs, and aligning OVC strategies with long-term investment goals and ESG considerations. Additionally, PE firms should prioritize collaboration and partnership, both within their portfolio and with external stakeholders, to leverage collective expertise and insights for value creation.

The future of OVC and OP engagement in the PE industry is poised for significant evolution, characterized by technological innovation, a focus on sustainable and impact-driven investment strategies, and the need for adaptive and versatile operational approaches. As PE firms navigate this landscape, strategic investments in OVC capabilities, talent development, and stakeholder collaboration will be key to unlocking new avenues for value creation and achieving sustained success in the dynamic world of private equity. Embracing these changes and leveraging the evolving role of OPs will ensure that PE firms remain at the forefront of driving transformative outcomes for their portfolio companies and the broader industry.

Deal Teams and Operating Partners: Compare and Contrast

In the multifaceted world of Private Equity (PE), the distinction between Deal Teams and Operational Value Creation (OVC) Teams, including the crucial role of Operational Partners (OPs), underscores the diverse strategies and approaches employed within the industry. This concluding section offers a comparative analysis of these pivotal entities, shedding light on their unique characteristics, working formats, interaction styles, and lifecycle of engagement.

Work Format

Deal Teams: Operate within a highly collaborative and structured environment, akin to lion prides. Their strength lies in unity, where each member's contribution is vital to the collective success of sourcing, evaluating, and executing deals. The teamwork-oriented approach facilitates the sharing of insights, risks, and rewards, fostering a dynamic learning environment where members grow and evolve through collective experience.

OVC Teams and OPs: Contrastingly, operate with a level of independence reminiscent of tigers. These seasoned professionals, often with extensive industry and operational expertise, navigate their roles with a degree of autonomy rarely seen in Deal Teams. Their work is characterized by direct interventions and hands-on management within portfolio companies, allowing them to implement transformative changes and drive value creation from within.

Interaction Style

Deal Teams: Engage in extensive interactions with a wide array of stakeholders, including investors, target company management, advisors, and intermediaries. Their role necessitates a diplomatic and influential interaction style, where consensus building, and negotiation skills are paramount. The need to navigate through multiple committees and approval gates before finalizing decisions underscores the importance of influence and strategic communication within their operational model.

OVC Teams and OPs: Exhibit a more authoritative and decisive interaction style, reflective of their mandate to implement operational improvements and strategic initiatives. Their engagement, often with the senior management of portfolio companies, demands a direct and assertive approach, enabling them to effectuate immediate and impactful changes. This interaction style is facilitated by their extensive experience and deep understanding of operational dynamics, granting them the credibility to lead with authority.

Lifecycle of Engagement

Deal Teams: Embark on a continuous journey of deal sourcing, execution, and portfolio management, with members participating in various stages of the investment lifecycle. This perpetual cycle offers Deal Team members opportunities for professional growth and learning, allowing them to accumulate a wealth of experience across different sectors and transaction types.

OVC Teams and OPs: Their engagement is typically more episodic, centered around specific operational challenges or strategic initiatives within portfolio companies. This focused involvement allows OPs to delve deeply into the nuances of a business, driving significant transformations within a finite timeframe. The lifecycle of their engagement is often defined by the achievement of predetermined value creation milestones or the successful exit from an investment.

Takeaway
The dichotomy between Deal Teams and OVC Teams, including OPs, within PE encapsulates the complex and complementary nature of investment and value creation in the industry. While Deal Teams are the strategists, navigating the intricacies of deal-making and stakeholder management, OVC Teams and OPs are the tacticians, effecting tangible improvements and strategic shifts within portfolio companies. This compare and contrast analysis not only highlights the distinct roles and operational styles of each group but also underscores the synergistic potential when these entities collaborate towards a common goal: maximizing the value and success of PE investments.

Section 3: Leadership Excellence in Private Equity

Understanding leadership in Private Equity

Understanding leadership in Private Equity (PE) requires a nuanced grasp of the unique environment within which these leaders operate. Unlike traditional corporate leadership, and whether on Deal Teams or Operating Partners, PE leadership involves navigating a landscape marked by high stakes, rapid transformations, and an unyielding focus on value creation within a finite time frame. This section delves into the complexities of leadership in PE, highlighting the distinct challenges and opportunities it presents, influenced by the economic landscape and emerging trends such as digitization and sustainability.

Proof in The Pudding

I would argue that PE professionals are far too busy and pragmatic to overthink Leadership as an in-depth concept. For them it is like asking a fish to explain swimming or a bird to describe flying. Whether great at it or not, every single PE player naturally leads in a way. This reminds or the most basic definition of Leadership:

"Leadership is Success; and Success is Leadership."

For PE Professionals, it is the outcome that best describe the skill. "The Proof is in the Pudding." And in the PE Pudding, the Investors' pallet counts most. It is even simple: Numbers. A whole track record of great numbers; that is Leadership!

Unique Challenges in PE Leadership

PE leaders are tasked with steering portfolio companies toward significant EBITDA growth, often within tightly defined strategic boundaries and an investment horizon that typically spans 3-7 years. This necessitates a leadership approach that is both strategic and hands-on, capable of driving operational improvements, fostering innovation, and executing swift pivots in response to market and technological changes.

1. **Intense Focus on Value Creation**: The primary goal is not just growth but sustainable value creation, which requires a deep understanding of the business, its market position, and the levers for improving performance and profitability.

2. **Strategic Decision-Making within Tight Boundaries**: PE leaders often work within the strategic confines set by the investment thesis, requiring a balance between long-term vision and short-term operational goals.

3. **Time-Bound Nature of Investments**: The finite investment period pressures leaders to achieve quick wins while setting the stage for enduring success, necessitating efficient prioritization and execution of strategic initiatives.

Navigating the Global Economy and Disruptive Trends

The global economic landscape and disruptive trends add layers of complexity to the role of PE leadership:

1. **Global Economic Fluctuations**: Leaders must steer portfolio companies through the uncertainties of global markets, including economic downturns, geopolitical tensions, and regulatory changes.

2. **Digitization**: Embracing digital transformation is no longer optional; it is a strategic imperative. PE leaders must ensure their portfolio companies leverage technology to enhance operations, customer experiences, and business models (Digital Operating Partners)

3. **Sustainability**: With increasing emphasis on ESG factors, leaders are tasked with integrating sustainable practices into the core strategy, not only to meet regulatory and investor expectations but also to drive long-term value.

The Digital Operating Partner (DOP)

AI & Automation Strategy

Implements data-driven optimization for portfolio management and decision-making processes.

Digital Transformation Execution

Leads technology integration efforts within portfolio companies to enhance overall performance.

Predictive Analytics

Leverages AI for real-time performance tracking, identifying trends, and advising on strategic actions.

Risk Management & Compliance

Utilizes advanced algorithms for fraud detection, cybersecurity, and regulatory compliance monitoring.

Leadership Skills for Success in PE

Successful PE leaders exhibit a blend of strategic vision, operational expertise, and adaptability, underpinned by a robust understanding of finance. They are adept at managing stakeholder relationships, motivating teams, and fostering a culture of excellence and innovation. Effective communication, resilience in the face of challenges, and the ability to drive change are crucial.

In sum, leadership in Private Equity is characterized by its focus on rapid, value-driven outcomes, necessitating a leadership style that is dynamic, strategic, and adaptable to both the pressures of the investment cycle and the evolving global business environment. As PE continues to evolve, leaders who can navigate these complexities while driving sustainable growth will be best positioned to succeed.

The Role of the PE Leader

The role of a Private Equity (PE) leader encompasses various critical facets, deeply ingrained in the essence of PE investment strategies and management philosophies. These leaders are not only required to possess an acute understanding of financial and strategic dynamics but also to embody a set of leadership qualities that are particularly pivotal in the high-stakes environment of PE.

Influential Leadership: PE leaders must wield influence effectively, aligning diverse groups of stakeholders around common goals. Their ability to shape strategies, influence outcomes, and drive consensus is crucial for navigating the complexities of PE investments.

Integrity of Thought: Decision-making in PE is often fraught with ambiguity and high pressure. Leaders must demonstrate integrity in their thought process, ensuring that every decision is made with a clear, ethical compass and is in the best interest of the investment and stakeholders.

Motivation and Inspiration: The nature of PE investments demands a leader who can inspire and motivate teams, often through periods of intense change and transformation. The ability to foster a culture of excellence and commitment is essential for achieving ambitious goals.

Team Collaboration: Success in PE is seldom the result of individual effort. It necessitates collaborative teamwork, where the leader plays a pivotal role in orchestrating efforts, managing dynamics, and leveraging the collective strengths of the team.

Matchmaking Skills: PE leaders excel in creating synergies, whether it is matching the right investment with the right strategy, aligning companies with potential partners, or connecting capital with opportunities. Their ability to identify and forge productive relationships is a key driver of value creation.

Visionary Outlook: PE leaders are often tasked with seeing beyond the present, envisioning the potential of a desert, and transforming it into a flourishing landscape. Their visionary outlook enables them to identify opportunities where others see challenges.

Optimism and Ambition: Inherent in the role of a PE leader is an optimistic view of the future, combined with the ambition to achieve remarkable outcomes. This optimism is not naive but grounded in realistic assessments and a relentless drive towards growth and success.

Lateral Thinking: The due diligence and management of investments require a leader to think across multiple domains—strategic, commercial, legal, and beyond. This ability to integrate diverse perspectives into coherent strategies is crucial for navigating the multifaceted challenges of PE investments.

Focus on Gain: At the core of every PE leader's mindset is an unwavering focus on financial gain and value creation. This focus informs every decision, strategy, and action, driving towards maximizing returns and achieving financial success.

Principal Mindset: PE leaders treat invested capital with the utmost respect and responsibility, embodying a principal mindset that instills a prominent level of accountability and stewardship. This approach ensures that investments are managed with the care and diligence they deserve.

In summary, the role of a PE leader is multifaceted, demanding a unique blend of strategic insight, ethical integrity, motivational prowess, and financial acumen. As the PE landscape continues to evolve, these leaders will play an increasingly critical role in steering investments toward unprecedented success, embodying the qualities that define exceptional leadership in the demanding world of Private Equity.

The NBA Talent Scout Analogy

The leadership in Private Equity (PE) can be likened to the role of talent scouts and coaches in the NBA. Just as scouts identify promising young talents with the potential to become basketball stars, PE deal teams seek out companies with untapped potential for growth and profitability. Similarly, Operational Partners (OPs) mirror the role of coaches, who take these talents under their wing, refining their skills, instilling discipline, and maximizing their performance on the court. In this analogy, the investment in potential and talent represents the financial and strategic investment in companies, with the goal of developing them to their full potential for a winning season, or in the case of PE, a successful exit strategy. These creative parallel highlights the dynamic roles within PE, emphasizing the strategic foresight, risk-taking, and developmental focus inherent in both fields.

Building and Leading High-Performing Deal Teams

Building and leading high-performing deal teams in private equity (PE) is a major challenge and undertaking akin to assembling and coaching a premier sports team. It is the foundation of all remarkable things that are built on top of it: performance, excellence, reputation, fundraising, fund deployment, value creation, repeat investors, etc.

The process goes beyond mere talent acquisition; it involves nurturing a culture of excellence, fostering collaborative dynamics, and instilling a shared commitment to achieving the investment thesis. Effective PE leaders recognize the importance of diversity in skills and perspectives, ensuring the team is well-rounded and equipped to navigate the complexities of PE investments. They empower team members, encourage autonomy within the framework of accountability, and focus on developing leaders who can continue the firm's legacy of success. The cultivation of strong relationships with limited partners and other stakeholders is also crucial, as these connections can provide a competitive edge in sourcing deals and securing capital.

To become fluent in building and leading high-performing deal teams in private equity (PE), it is essential to consider various facets of leadership and team dynamics. This requires profound understanding of key themes, each addressing critical elements of effective team building and leadership within the PE context.

Foundations of High-Performing Teams:

Building high-performing teams in Private Equity (PE) is a nuanced endeavor that requires a strategic approach to leadership. A foundational element of such teams is the diversity in skills and perspectives, which enriches problem-solving and decision-making processes. This diversity not only brings a wide range of insights but also fosters a culture of innovation and collaboration. Effective PE leaders understand the importance of creating an environment that encourages team members to voice their opinions and ideas freely, thereby enhancing the team's ability to tackle complex challenges and seize new opportunities. This environment, where psychological safety is prioritized, is crucial for nurturing high-performing teams that can drive the firm's success in the competitive PE landscape.

Leadership Qualities for PE Success:

Leadership in Private Equity (PE) necessitates qualities that go beyond conventional business leadership. Visionary thinking allows leaders to foresee potential outcomes and guide their teams and investments towards long-term success. The ability to influence and inspire is crucial for rallying teams around shared goals and maintaining high morale, even in challenging times. Integrity ensures that decisions are made with honesty and transparency, fostering trust among team members, investors, and stakeholders. A results-driven approach focuses on achieving specific objectives, emphasizing the importance of measurable outcomes in PE investments.

In the PE context, leaders also excel as matchmakers, adeptly connecting capital with lucrative opportunities, aligning talent with strategic needs, and facilitating synergies that maximize investment value. This role is essential for navigating the complex landscape of PE investments, where the right connections can significantly impact the success of a deal.

Strategic and Tactical Leadership:

Private Equity (PE) leaders must adeptly toggle between strategic and tactical leadership to balance ambitious goals with practical execution strategies. This duality is essential because it ensures that visionary objectives are grounded in actionable steps that can be realistically implemented. Strategic leadership allows PE leaders to set long-term goals and directions, envisioning future possibilities and growth avenues. Simultaneously, tactical leadership focuses on the day-to-day operations and the meticulous execution of plans, ensuring that the strategic vision is translated into tangible results. This approach enables PE leaders to drive their firms and portfolio companies towards achieving high-stakes investment theses while navigating the complexities and rapid changes of the financial markets. Balancing these aspects is crucial for maintaining a competitive edge and achieving sustained success in the dynamic PE landscape.

Cultivating a Culture of Excellence:

Private Equity (PE) leaders foster a culture of efficiency, accountability, and continuous improvement, drawing inspiration from highly organized systems like ant colonies. In such environments, each member knows their role and diligently contributes towards achieving common objectives. This analogy reflects the structured yet flexible nature of PE firms, where leadership emphasizes clear roles, responsibilities, and expectations. By instilling these values, PE leaders create an ecosystem where every team member is empowered to excel, innovate, and drive the firm towards its strategic goals, mirroring the collective effort and efficiency observed in the natural world.

Building and Sustaining Relationships:

Private Equity (PE) leaders play a pivotal role in fostering a culture of excellence, collaboration, and innovation within their firms and portfolio companies. They are instrumental in nurturing relationships with limited partners and stakeholders, ensuring long-term success and creating a brand of excellence that transcends individual achievements. Through strategic leadership, PE leaders build high-performing teams, align talent management with the investment thesis, and balance ambitious goals with practical execution strategies. They also emphasize efficiency, accountability, and continuous improvement, drawing parallels to well-organized systems where each member contributes towards a common goal. By being visionary, influential, and integrity-driven, PE leaders not only drive financial success but also establish a legacy of transformative leadership within the private equity sector.

Each of the elements above is paramount to better understanding the multifaceted role of PE leaders in building teams that are not just skilled in executing transactions but also in driving sustainable growth and creating value across the investment lifecycle. Besides the above PE Leadership requirements, one key leadership attribute stands out as crucial to the success of PE Teams: <u>Adaptive Leadership</u>.

Adaptive Leadership as a Strategy in Private Equity

Adaptive leadership in private equity (PE) is crucial for navigating the fast-paced and uncertain investment landscape. This leadership style emphasizes flexibility, empathy, and the ability to lead through change. Adaptive PE leaders are like talent scouts, identifying and nurturing potential to build a competitive edge. They balance strategic vision with practical execution, focusing on long-term gains and fostering a culture of innovation and accountability. This approach ensures PE firms can adapt to market shifts, technological advancements, and evolving global conditions, driving sustainable value creation and long-term success in the competitive world of private equity.

Dimensions of Adaptive Leadership

Adaptive leadership distinguishes itself in several ways, most notably through its focus on navigating business environments with uncertainty, leveraging diversity of perspectives, sharing leadership based on context, and constantly questioning the surrounding world to align organizations with shifting environments.

1. **Navigating Business Environment**: Adaptive leaders embrace uncertainty and adopt novel approaches to chart a course amid turbulent conditions. They manage the context of interactions rather than rigid rules, cultivating a diversity of perspectives to generate multiple options for action. This approach often involves

de-emphasizing hierarchy and allowing leadership to emerge from those best positioned to guide specific decisions.

2. **Leading with Empathy**: Creating a shared sense of purpose and managing through influence rather than command and control is crucial. Adaptive leaders see the world through others' eyes, embracing cognitive diversity and extending their ability to navigate complex environments.

3. **Learning Through Self-Correction**: Encouraging experimentation is key, with the understanding that some experiments will fail. This is how adaptive organizations learn. Leaders should develop platforms that enable experimentation and learning, align rewards with experimentation, and not punish failure.

4. **Creating Win-Win Solutions**: Adaptive leaders focus on sustainable success for both the company and its external network of stakeholders. They build platforms for collaboration and deploy leadership influence beyond the firm's boundaries, structuring for win-win outcomes.

Adaptive Strategies for PE Leaders

To embody adaptive leadership, PE leaders should empower and invest in adaptability to prepare for a fast-paced and uncertain future. This involves identifying root causes of challenges, course correcting, and anticipating future needs. Key strategies include cultivating compassionate leadership, solving the 'adaptability paradox' for long-term success, and integrating adaptability into leadership blueprints for growth.

In the context of PE, adaptive leadership translates into the ability to influence and inspire, maintain integrity of thought, and drive results within tightly defined strategic boundaries and time-bound nature of investments. It is about building winning teams, empowering success, and creating a franchise that goes beyond individual achievements to establish a brand name recognized for excellence and integrity.

Adaptive leadership in PE also means balancing ambitious goals with practical execution strategies, fostering a culture of efficiency and accountability, and nurturing relationships with limited partners and stakeholders to ensure long-term success. This approach ensures that PE firms remain agile, innovative, and capable of leading through periods of uncertainty and change.

By focusing on these adaptive leadership strategies, PE leaders can ensure their firms and portfolio companies are well-positioned to navigate the complexities of the investment landscape, drive sustainable value creation, and achieve long-term success in the competitive world of private equity.

A well-built PE team operates with precision and unity, much like an ant colony where each member plays a critical role towards a common goal. There is a sense of pride in their work, a drive to excel, and a recognition that the team's success is intrinsically linked to their collective efforts. Leadership in this context is about enabling others to succeed, creating an environment where innovation is nurtured, and every challenge is met with determination and strategic insight.

Navigating People Challenges and Risks in PE Leadership

Navigating Challenges and Risks in PE Leadership focuses on the intricacies of managing the human aspects of business operations within Private Equity (PE) investments. This entails a comprehensive approach toward understanding and enhancing the human capital, leadership effectiveness, and cultural integration with and of portfolio companies. Key areas include the importance of human capital due diligence to uncover potential talent and leadership gaps, and the evaluation of leadership effectiveness to ensure strategic execution and strategies for successful cultural integration post-acquisition. Additionally, it addresses the significance of talent retention to maintain business stability and growth, alongside effective change management to facilitate smooth transitions. Leadership succession planning is highlighted as a critical component for ensuring continuity and long-term success. Addressing these challenges requires strategic insight and a proactive approach to managing the complexities associated with human capital in PE investments.

Accordingly, we can focus on the PE oversight of the Portfolio Companies Human Capital and cover 6 distinct areas:

1. **Human Capital Due Diligence**: This critical phase demands a comprehensive assessment of the team's capabilities, leadership qualities, and overall alignment with the PE firm's strategic vision. Failure to accurately

evaluate these factors can lead to significant post-acquisition challenges, underscoring the importance of a meticulous due diligence process to uncover potential talent gaps or cultural misalignments that could impact the investment's success.

2. **Leadership Effectiveness**: The effectiveness of leadership within portfolio companies is a determinant of their growth and operational efficiency. Weak leadership can significantly impede these areas, making it vital for PE leaders to assess and enhance existing leadership capabilities to ensure they are conducive to strategic execution and organizational alignment.

3. **Cultural Integration**: The merging of disparate organizational cultures following an acquisition presents a complex challenge. Cultural clashes can lead to operational disruptions and employee demotivation, highlighting the necessity for strategies that facilitate smooth cultural integration to maintain a cohesive and productive workforce.

4. **Talent Retention**: Retaining key talent post-acquisition is paramount for maintaining operational continuity and fostering growth. The risk of losing essential personnel necessitates implementing effective talent retention strategies to safeguard against disruptions that could derail the investment's objectives.

5. **Change Management**: Successfully managing organizational changes with minimal disruption is a crucial competency for PE leaders. Poorly executed change management can result in resistance and productivity losses, emphasizing the need for carefully planned and communicated change initiatives that align with the company's strategic goals.

6. **Leadership Succession Planning**: The identification and development of future leaders are essential for ensuring the long-term success and stability of portfolio companies. A lack of succession planning can lead to leadership voids, making it imperative for PE firms to proactively address this aspect to secure a seamless transition and continuity of leadership.

The same six areas covered above should also be meticulously planned and executed within the PE Teams themselves, albeit with a more subtle and structured approach. I would argue that the hiring process for PE team are so rigorous and demanding for a reason and PE General Partners go to great lengths to validate the competency, fit and long-term outlook of any hire into their midst.

Streamlining Steadfast Leadership during Crisis, Challenge and Change

The 3 C's of PE Normal

Leadership in times of uncertainty and change is a defining characteristic of private equity (PE) professionals, who often operate under high stakes and pressure. Their work environment is rife with challenges such as tight deadlines, complex deal negotiations, and the need for rapid adjustments to unforeseen market shifts. This constant state of flux demands a leadership style that is not only adaptable but also visionary, capable of steering firms and investments through turbulence with strategic foresight and resilience.

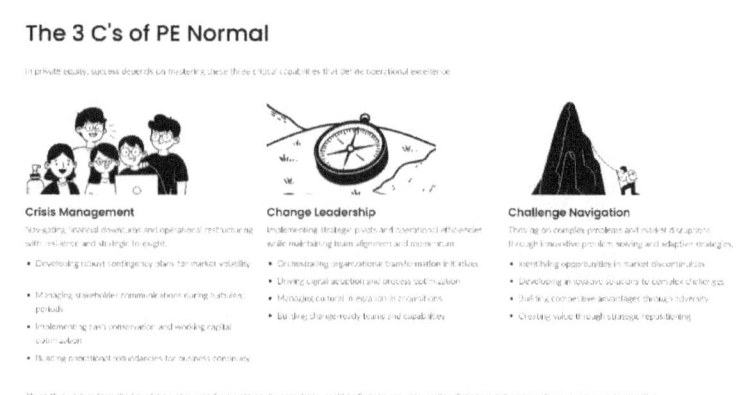

PE leaders excel in crisis management, drawing on a deep well of experience in navigating financial downturns, operational restructuring, and stakeholder disputes. Their ability to remain calm under pressure, make decisive actions based on thorough risk assessment, and maintain a sharp vision for the future positions them as adept navigators of the unpredictable business landscape. This adaptability is enhanced by their expertise in assembling high-performing teams that share a commitment to achieving investment objectives, despite the uncertainties.

Moreover, the very nature of PE investment strategies—focused on transforming and improving portfolio companies—equips PE leaders with a unique set of tools and approaches for managing change. They are skilled in implementing strategic pivots and operational efficiencies that not only safeguard investments during downturns but also capitalize on opportunities that emerge from market disruptions.

In essence, the turbulent business environment in which PE operates serves as a proving ground for leadership qualities that thrive on challenge and change. PE leaders' adeptness at crisis management, strategic adaptability, and fostering a culture of resilience and innovation underscores their role as pivotal agents of change, capable of leading their firms and portfolio companies to sustained success in an ever-evolving market landscape.

In more eloquent terms, PE pushes its staff and team members - whether Deal Teams or Operating Partners - to their mortal limits and expects them to juggle at every juncture of the PE lifecycle - from scouting deals to exit and every stage in between:

1. The High-Stakes Arena

- **Pressure Cooker Environment**: PE professionals operate in a high-stakes arena where every decision reverberates across portfolios, investors, and markets. The clock ticks relentlessly, demanding swift and strategic moves.

- **Deal Dynamics**: From due diligence to exit strategies, PE leaders orchestrate intricate deals. They must assess risks, evaluate potential, and align investments with long-term visions.

2. The Art of Crisis Management

- **Calm Amid Chaos**: PE leaders thrive under pressure. Their ability to maintain composure during market downturns, industry disruptions, or unexpected events is akin to a seasoned captain steering a ship through a storm.

- **Decisiveness**: In the face of uncertainty, PE leaders make tough calls. They analyze data, consult experts, and act swiftly. Their decisions ripple through organizations, affecting employees, investors, and stakeholders.

3. Visionary Adaptability

- **Navigating the Unknown**: PE leaders are not just reactive; they are visionaries. They anticipate shifts, spot trends, and adapt strategies. Their agility allows them to pivot when markets twist unexpectedly.

- **Strategic Foresight**: PE leaders peer into the fog of uncertainty and discern patterns. They see beyond immediate challenges, envisioning a future where investments flourish.

4. The Team Architects

- **Assembling Dream Teams**: PE leaders know that success hinges on talent. They scout, recruit, and nurture high-performing teams. These teams share a common purpose: maximizing returns.

- **Culture Catalysts**: PE leaders foster a culture of excellence. They instill discipline, accountability, and a hunger for results. Their teams become engines of transformation.

5. The PE Playbook: Change Agents

- **Operational Alchemists**: PE leaders wield a playbook that transforms companies. They optimize operations, streamline processes, and unlock hidden value. Their magic lies in turning complexity into simplicity.
- **Capitalizing on Disruption**: PE leaders do not fear change; they embrace it. Market shifts become opportunities. They reposition portfolio companies, leveraging disruption to their advantage.

6. Resilience and Innovation

- **The Resilience Quotient**: PE leaders bounce back from setbacks. They learn from failures, adapt, and forge ahead. Their resilience fuels reinvention.
- **Innovators at Heart**: PE leaders are restless innovators. They challenge conventions, experiment, and reimagine business models. Their hunger for improvement is insatiable.

7. The Legacy Architects

- **Beyond the Deal**: PE leaders think beyond transactions. They envision legacies—companies transformed, industries disrupted, and communities impacted.
- **Stewards of Capital**: PE leaders honor their fiduciary duty. They manage investors' capital with care, aiming for sustainable growth and lasting impact.

To Lead in PE is to be the Mantra, Mentor and Mentee

The 3 M's of PE Values

To effectively lead in Private Equity (PE), adopting the roles of mentor, mentee, and mantra-bearer is crucial. This multifaceted approach ensures leaders not only guide others but also seek growth through learning from peers and mentors. Mentorship in PE is about passing down wisdom and experiences, helping to navigate the sector's complexities. Coaching focuses on unlocking individual potential and addressing specific challenges, fostering a culture of continuous improvement and professional development. Great PE leaders prioritize creating a mentorship ecosystem, ensuring every team member both learns from and contributes to the collective knowledge pool. Additionally, embodying and sharing core professional values strengthen team alignment and investment success, making mentorship and coaching indispensable for sustaining firm growth and adaptability in the dynamic PE industry.

Teach, Learn and Inspire None-Stop

This comprehensive approach to leadership fosters a culture of continuous growth, knowledge sharing, and aligned values within the firm.

The Mentor

In the role of mentor, a PE leader guides, advises, and supports less experienced colleagues, sharing insights from their own journey. This mentorship extends beyond professional development to include advice on navigating the intricacies of PE transactions, strategic decision-making, and career advancement. It is a commitment to nurturing the next generation of leaders by providing them with the tools, confidence, and wisdom needed to excel.

The Mentee

Even as leaders, staying open to learning is crucial. As a mentee, a PE leader seeks guidance and perspectives from more experienced professionals, demonstrating humility and a continuous desire for personal and professional development. This role reinforces the importance of lifelong learning and the belief that everyone has something valuable to teach us, regardless of their position or tenure.

The Mantra-Bearer

PE leaders are also mantra-bearers, embodying and promoting core professional values and principles that define the firm's culture and operational philosophy. These mantras could revolve around integrity, diligence, innovation, or resilience, serving as a compass for the firm's strategic direction and decision-making processes. By living these values, leaders inspire their teams to adopt and uphold the same standards, creating a cohesive and principled workforce.

The 3 M's of PE Values

In the dynamic world of Private Equity, success is built on a foundation of strong professional values and continuous development. These three key principles form the cornerstone of excellence in PE leadership and organizational culture.

1	2	3
Mentor	**Mentee**	**Mantra-Bearer**
Guiding and supporting less experienced colleagues	Seeking guidance and perspectives for continuous growth	Embodying and promoting core professional values
• Share industry expertise	• Demonstrate commitment to learning	• Maintain high ethical standards
• Provide strategic guidance	• Remain open to new perspectives	• Promote transparency
• Offer constructive feedback	• Actively seek feedback	• Foster culture of excellence

These three roles work together in a continuous cycle of growth and development. While individuals may primarily occupy one role at a time, successful PE leaders often move fluidly between all three positions, creating a dynamic environment of continuous learning and professional development.

The 7-Step Roadmap to Mastering PE-Wisdom Leadership

This is my own cheat sheet to Leadership introspection and self-training.

The **7-Step Roadmap to Mastering PE-Wisdom Leadership** integrates key principles of personal leadership development with the unique demands of Private Equity (PE) leadership. This roadmap provides a structured approach for PE professionals to enhance their leadership skills and impact, and a guiding framework for outsiders who like to gain insights from the PE challenging environment to improve their leadership introspection and refinement.

Mastering PE Wisdom to Enhance Your Leadership Style

This section is a suggested personal self-help life coach in print – the 7 Steps Roadmap to Leadership Mastery taking stock of PE experience and Wisdom. Designed for specialist PE practitioners or everyday individuals like you, this transformative guide will empower you to embark on a journey of self-discovery, growth, and empowerment.

Step 1: Embrace Self-Discovery and be a Life-Learner

- Always assume that you do not know it all! And that knowledge will further empower your success. Adopt A Life learner style regardless of your position or paycheck.

- Ground your ego. Explore your strengths, weaknesses, values, and aspirations through self-reflection and introspection, and on a regular basis.

- Seek feedback from trusted peers, mentors, and colleagues to gain valuable insights into areas for growth and improvement.

Step 2: Practice and Role Play – with a sense of Urgency!

- Engage in regular and time-critical practice and role-playing exercises to develop and refine your leadership skills in various scenarios.

- Create opportunities to simulate real-life leadership challenges and experiment with different approaches to problem-solving, crisis-management and decision-making.

Step 3: Be a Mentor - Be a Mentee - Embrace a Mantra

- Identify a mentor who can provide guidance, support, and wisdom based on their own experiences and expertise.

- Consider becoming a mentor to someone else, offering your insights and perspective while also learning from their unique experiences and perspectives.

- Always reflect on your professional values and practice to be that storyteller who speaks from the mind and heart: To Impact and To Inspire!

Step 4: Choose Your Personal Goals Carefully; BHAG Yourself

- Carefully select your "personal goals": Growth, Knowledge, Experiences, and a Person as well! Choose a leader whom you admire and aspire to emulate, studying their leadership style, values, and principles. You would be lucky if that person is your colleague or within your first-degree network.

- Treat your next better version of yourself as your own BHAG project. Aim high, think big, work hard!

- Conquer the hills toward your Mount BHAG!

Step 5: Think Principal; and Numbers

- Remember to act as a Principal in all your Deals and dealings; treat all resources as your own.

- You Are not an Agent; the only agent you would consider is that of Change!

- Success is not just words; success is a matter of numbers; know your numbers well! After all Leadership is Success.

Step 6: Think Principles; and Values

- Hold on to professional principles. Make sure you are equipped with the right principles and beyond the deal.

- Define early on what are your Do's and Don'ts;' Say and Say nots; adapt on pricing and never compromise on value.

- True Values Create Lasting Value

Step 7: Embrace, Enjoy and Reflect on the Journey

- Embrace the journey of self-discovery and growth with curiosity, openness, and a sense of adventure.

- Celebrate your progress and achievements along the way, while also recognizing that growth is a continuous and lifelong process.

By focusing on self-improvement and personal development, you can embark on a transformative journey toward becoming the best version of yourself as a leader and as an individual.

This roadmap encourages a blend of personal development, strategic learning, and practical experience, tailored to the demanding and dynamic environment of PE leadership.

Case Studies on Impactful and Adaptive PE Leadership

Case Study 1: The Rise of Vista Equity Partners – How Robert Smith Revolutionized Software Private Equity

Private equity has traditionally focused on industries like manufacturing, retail, and infrastructure. However, Robert Smith's **Vista Equity Partners** took a different approach—focusing exclusively on **enterprise software companies** and proving that technology-focused private equity could deliver **consistent, high-margin returns**. Vista's success reshaped the entire industry, forcing competitors to rethink how they approached technology investments.

Challenges: An Underserved Market in Private Equity

Before Vista was founded in **2000**, private equity firms largely overlooked **software businesses** due to their intangible assets and reliance on recurring revenue models. The industry lacked operational PE firms that could systematically improve software businesses. Smith saw an **opportunity to standardize and optimize enterprise software operations**, turning struggling or stagnant firms into industry leaders.

Strategic Execution: The Vista Playbook for Scaling Software Companies

Vista Equity Partners' success was **not accidental**—it was **built on a disciplined, repeatable playbook** for growing software businesses:

- **Operational Standardization:** Vista introduced **proprietary best practices** for running software companies efficiently, improving processes across sales, customer success, and engineering.

- **Focus on Recurring Revenue Models:** Vista specialized in **subscription-based SaaS models**, ensuring predictable revenue streams and higher profit margins.

- **Strategic Bolt-On Acquisitions:** The firm actively **merged and consolidated smaller software firms**, creating **platform businesses** that dominated niche markets.

- **Leadership Development:** Vista trained executives using **a rigorous, systematized approach**, ensuring management teams operated with the same principles across all portfolio companies.

Results: A Multi-Billion Dollar Software PE Giant

Vista Equity Partners rapidly grew into **one of the world's largest private equity firms** focused exclusively on technology, managing over **$100 billion in assets**. The firm successfully **scaled and exited multiple high-profile software companies**, including:

- **Marketo** – Acquired for **$1.8 billion**, later sold to Adobe for **$4.75 billion**.

- **Datto** – Bought for **$1.5 billion**, later went public at a **$4 billion valuation**.

- **SolarWinds** – Acquired and improved operationally, later exited through an **$8 billion IPO**.

Leadership Takeaways: The Power of a Repeatable Investment Strategy

Vista's rise under Robert Smith demonstrated that **private equity firms could build industry-specific playbooks and create massive value through operational discipline.** Instead of focusing on traditional LBO models, **Vista pioneered an active, systematic approach to software investing,** which is now widely copied by firms like Thoma Bravo and Silver Lake.

Case Study 2: Warburg Pincus and the Transformation of Avalara – Scaling a Tax Technology Leader

Warburg Pincus, one of the **oldest and most successful private equity firms**, has a strong track record of **growth investing** rather than relying on cost-cutting strategies. One of its biggest recent success stories is **Avalara**, a once-small tax compliance software company that Warburg helped scale into a dominant **$8 billion publicly traded company**.

Challenges: A Niche Market with Untapped Potential

When Warburg Pincus first invested in **Avalara** in **2014**, it was a **relatively small player in the sales tax automation space**. While its cloud-based tax compliance solution had potential, the company **lacked the scale, global reach, and enterprise credibility** to compete with giants like **SAP and Oracle** in financial software.

Strategic Execution: A Growth-Oriented PE Playbook

Instead of focusing on cost efficiencies, Warburg Pincus helped **Avalara scale aggressively**, using a combination of:

- **Market Expansion:** Pushed Avalara into **global markets**, expanding beyond the U.S. to help companies comply with international tax regulations.

- **Strategic Acquisitions:** Funded **more than 15 bolt-on acquisitions**, strengthening Avalara's product capabilities and market position.

- **Enterprise Sales Scaling:** Shifted Avalara's focus from **SMBs to large enterprises**, expanding into Fortune 500 clients.

- **IPO Readiness:** Positioned Avalara for a **highly successful IPO in 2018**, raising over **$300 million** and later reaching a market cap of **$8 billion** before being acquired by Vista Equity in 2022.

Results: A PE-Backed Growth Success Story

Warburg Pincus **helped Avalara expand its revenue by more than 400%** while dramatically improving its **profit margins and global reach**. Unlike turnaround-focused private equity strategies, this was a **growth-driven investment** where Warburg's capital and operational expertise helped Avalara dominate a rapidly growing fintech niche.

Leadership Takeaways: Scaling Through PE-Backed Expansion

Avalara's success underscores **how private equity is not just about cost-cutting—it can be a powerful enabler of growth.** Warburg Pincus showed that **patient capital, aggressive expansion, and strategic M&A** can be just as transformative as traditional restructuring.

Case Study 3: How EQT Transformed SUSE into a European Tech Powerhouse

EQT, one of Europe's largest private equity firms, has been a leader in **technology-focused investing**, helping **SUSE**, a German open-source enterprise software company, transition from an overlooked asset to a **publicly traded company valued at over $7 billion**.

Challenges: A Legacy Business in Need of a Digital Shift

When EQT acquired **SUSE from Micro Focus in 2018 for $2.5 billion**, the company was **profitable but underperforming**. While SUSE had strong open-source enterprise software products, it was struggling to **compete against larger firms like Red Hat and VMware** in the growing cloud computing space.

Strategic Execution: A High-Growth, PE-Led Digital Transformation

EQT's strategy to scale SUSE involved a **three-pronged approach**:

- **Accelerating Cloud Growth:** Shifted SUSE's focus from traditional on-premise software to **cloud-based solutions**, making it more competitive in the modern enterprise IT landscape.

- **Acquisitions to Strengthen Market Position:** Supported SUSE's **acquisition of Rancher Labs**, a leading Kubernetes company, to expand its cloud-native capabilities.

- **Operational Excellence & IPO Preparation:** Optimized operations, improved margins, and set SUSE up for a **high-profile IPO in 2021** at a valuation of **$7 billion**.

Results: Transforming a Legacy Software Firm into a High-Growth Public Company

- SUSE successfully **expanded into cloud and container-based solutions**, making it a **key player in the enterprise software space**.
- EQT helped **grow revenues significantly** while improving SUSE's operating efficiency.
- The **IPO was one of the largest tech exits in Europe**, proving the value of PE-led growth investments.

Leadership Takeaways: Adapting Legacy Companies for the Future

SUSE's transformation under EQT highlights how **PE firms can take traditional companies and reposition them for long-term success.** Rather than just extracting value, EQT's leadership focused on **innovation, strategic M&A, and positioning the company for a strong public debut.**

Final Thoughts on These Case Studies

Each of these case studies highlights a **different type of PE leadership strategy**:

1. **Vista Equity Partners (Robert Smith) – Driving Value Through Operational Excellence in Software**
2. **Warburg Pincus (Avalara) – Scaling a High-Growth Fintech Business Through Expansion & Acquisitions**
3. **EQT (SUSE) – Modernizing a Legacy Software Firm for a Digital Future**

These cases show that **private equity leadership is not just about cutting costs—it's about strategic capital deployment, operational discipline, and unlocking new growth opportunities.**

Appendix

Examples on Primary and Secondary Leadership Qualities

This table below highlights leaders from various industries who exemplify the primary and secondary qualities of effective leadership. Each leader's accomplishments illustrate how they embody these traits in their leadership roles.

Trait	Leader and Accomplishment
Vision	Angela Ahrendts, former Senior Vice President of Apple Retail, demonstrated exceptional vision by transforming Apple's retail stores into vibrant community spaces. Under her leadership, Apple stores became more than just places to buy products; they became hubs for creativity, learning, and connection. Ahrendts' vision emphasized the importance of human interaction in the digital age, leading to innovative store designs and immersive experiences that redefined retail.
Integrity	Bob Iger, former CEO of The Walt Disney Company, exemplified integrity by leading Disney through a period of expansion and transformation with honesty and authenticity. Iger's commitment to upholding Disney's legacy while embracing

	innovation and diversity earned him respect from employees, shareholders, and audiences worldwide. His integrity was evident in his strategic decisions, such as the acquisition of Pixar, Marvel, and Lucasfilm, which fueled Disney's growth and success.
Communication	Reed Hastings, co-founder, and CEO of Netflix demonstrated exceptional communication skills by revolutionizing the way people consume entertainment. Hastings effectively communicated Netflix's vision of disrupting the traditional media landscape, leading to the widespread adoption of streaming services worldwide. His transparent and bold communication style, coupled with Netflix's innovative content strategy, transformed the entertainment industry and reshaped consumer behavior.
Trust	Mary Dillon, former CEO of Ulta Beauty, earned trust by leading the company through shifts in consumer preferences and retail trends. Dillon's strategic initiatives, including expanding Ulta's product offerings and enhancing the in-store experience, positioned the company for success in the evolving beauty industry. Her ability to anticipate and respond to changes in the market enabled Ulta to maintain its competitive edge and drive sustainable growth.

Organization	Tim Armstrong, former CEO of AOL, demonstrated exceptional organizational skills by leading the company through a period of transformation in the digital media industry. Under his leadership, AOL diversified its business beyond internet services, acquiring companies like The Huffington Post and TechCrunch to expand its content offerings. Armstrong's strategic initiatives and focus on innovation revitalized AOL's brand and positioned it as a leading player in online media and advertising.
Resilience	Sundar Pichai, CEO of Alphabet Inc. (Google), exemplified resilience by navigating Google through complex challenges and technological disruptions. Pichai's leadership during times of regulatory scrutiny, privacy concerns, and market volatility highlighted his ability to adapt and persevere in the face of adversity. His strategic vision and commitment to innovation enabled Google to maintain its position as a leading technology company and drive long-term value for stakeholders.
Innovation	Sheryl Sandberg, COO of Meta Platforms (formerly Facebook), demonstrated exceptional innovation by shaping the growth and evolution of social media and digital advertising. Sandberg's leadership at Facebook focused on expanding the platform's user base and monetization

	strategies while promoting initiatives like Facebook's Diversity and Inclusion efforts and Lean In. Her advocacy for women in leadership and technology contributed to greater diversity and innovation within the industry.
Adaptability	Jensen Huang, co-founder, and CEO of NVIDIA showcased adaptability by leading the company through rapid technological advancements and market shifts in the semiconductor industry. Huang's strategic focus on artificial intelligence and GPU computing positioned NVIDIA as a leader in high-performance computing and AI acceleration. His ability to pivot the company's strategy and product portfolio enabled NVIDIA to capitalize on emerging opportunities and drive sustained growth.
Courage	Rosalind Brewer, former CEO of Sam's Club, and current CEO of Walgreens Boots Alliance demonstrated courage by championing diversity, equity, and inclusion initiatives in corporate leadership. Brewer's advocacy for gender and racial diversity in executive positions challenged traditional norms and promoted a more inclusive workplace culture. Her courage to address systemic barriers and drive organizational change earned her recognition as a trailblazer in the retail industry and beyond.

Accountability	Dara Khosrowshahi, CEO of Uber, embraced accountability by leading the company through a period of transformation and cultural change. Khosrowshahi's focus on transparency, ethical business practices, and corporate governance restored trust in Uber's brand and reputation. His commitment to accountability and integrity in decision-making fostered a culture of responsibility and accountability among employees, investors, and stakeholders.
Relationships	Doug McMillon, CEO of Walmart, prioritized relationships by investing in employees, customers, and communities to drive sustainable growth and social impact. McMillon's focus on building trust and fostering collaboration with stakeholders strengthened Walmart's reputation as a responsible corporate citizen. His commitment to empowering associates, supporting small businesses, and addressing societal challenges reinforced Walmart's role as a leader in retail and social responsibility.
Empowerment	Brian Chesky, co-founder and CEO of Airbnb, empowered hosts, and travelers worldwide by creating a platform that revolutionized the hospitality industry. Chesky's vision for Airbnb as a community-driven marketplace empowered individuals to share their spaces and experiences, fostering connections and cultural

	exchange. His commitment to empowering hosts with tools and support enabled Airbnb to scale globally and redefine travel and accommodations.
Servant	Hubert Joly, former CEO of Best Buy, embodied servant leadership by prioritizing the well-being of employees, customers, and communities. Joly's customer-centric approach and employee empowerment initiatives, such as the "Renew Blue" turnaround strategy, revitalized Best Buy's business and culture. His commitment to serving stakeholders with humility, empathy, and integrity transformed Best Buy into a customer-focused and socially responsible retailer.

Case Studies of Inspirational and Exceptional PE Leadership

Case 1: Henry Kravis & George Roberts – Pioneering the Leveraged Buyout

Why?
Few figures in Private Equity have had as profound an impact as Henry Kravis and George Roberts, the co-founders of **Kohlberg Kravis Roberts & Co. (KKR)**. Their leadership and innovation in leveraged buyouts (LBOs) redefined the industry and set new standards for dealmaking, financial structuring, and value creation.

Who?
Henry Kravis and George Roberts, cousins and former investment bankers, co-founded KKR in 1976 alongside Jerome Kohlberg. Their approach to financing corporate acquisitions through high levels of debt changed the landscape of private equity and became the blueprint for modern buyouts.

When?
Their defining moment came in **1988** when KKR executed **the landmark acquisition of RJR Nabisco for $31.1 billion**, one of the largest and most complex LBOs in history. The deal became legendary, inspiring the book *Barbarians at the Gate* and symbolizing the aggressive yet strategic nature of private equity investing.

What Did They Do?

Kravis and Roberts popularized **financial engineering** as a core PE strategy. They identified undervalued companies, acquired them using **highly leveraged debt**, and then focused on **operational efficiencies, cost reductions, and strategic growth** before selling them at a premium. Their leadership style involved:

- **Aligning investor and management incentives** to drive performance.
- **Taking an active role in company restructuring** to create long-term value.
- **Innovating capital structures** that allowed massive acquisitions with minimal equity contributions.

Legacy:
KKR's leadership transformed **private equity from a niche investment strategy into a global powerhouse.** Today, LBOs are the backbone of private equity transactions, and their dealmaking playbook is still widely followed. Kravis and Roberts' emphasis on **strategic execution, operational value creation, and disciplined financial structuring** remains a model for modern PE leaders.

Case 2: Robert Smith – Building a Tech-Focused PE Empire

Why?

Robert F. Smith, founder of **Vista Equity Partners**, revolutionized private equity by applying a **technology-first approach** to investing. While many PE firms traditionally focused on industrials and consumer businesses, Smith **recognized the untapped value in enterprise software and technology companies**, positioning Vista as a dominant force in this sector.

Who?

Born in 1962, Smith started as a chemical engineer before transitioning into investment banking at Goldman Sachs. In **2000, he founded Vista Equity Partners**, focusing exclusively on software, a decision that would make Vista one of the **most successful private equity firms of the 21st century**.

When?

Vista's rise to prominence accelerated in **2010-2020**, as it became the premier investor in enterprise software companies, executing **over 500 software deals** and building an asset base exceeding **$100 billion**.

What Did He Do?

Smith's leadership at Vista Equity was unique in that he introduced **a rigorous, standardized approach to operating software businesses**, known as the **Vista Best Practices framework**. This methodology focused on:

- **Systematic operational improvements** in portfolio companies.
- **Data-driven performance tracking** to optimize efficiency.
- **Long-term growth strategies** instead of quick exits.

This model helped Vista transform underperforming software companies into **high-margin, high-growth enterprises**.

Legacy:

Smith's leadership transformed **Vista Equity Partners into the largest private equity firm dedicated to software investments**. His success also **paved the way for tech-focused private equity**, influencing firms like Silver Lake and Thoma Bravo. Additionally, Smith is known for his philanthropy, including **paying off student loans for an entire graduating class at Morehouse College in 2019**.

Case 3: Orlando Bravo – The "Godfather of Software Private Equity"

Why?

Orlando Bravo, co-founder and managing partner of **Thoma Bravo**, has been a key figure in **redefining private equity's approach to software investing**. He pioneered **the aggressive consolidation of software companies** and built **one of the most successful PE firms in the world.**

Who?

Born in Puerto Rico, Bravo attended Brown University and Stanford Law & Business School. After working in investment banking, he co-led Thoma Bravo's shift toward **buying, scaling, and integrating software companies.**

When?

Thoma Bravo's defining era began in the **2010s**, when the firm began executing **mega deals in enterprise software**, acquiring companies like McAfee, SolarWinds, and Instructure.

What Did He Do?

Bravo's leadership transformed **Thoma Bravo into a PE powerhouse** by:

- **Acquiring software companies and merging them into high-performing platforms.**
- **Implementing operational efficiencies** to scale revenue and profit margins.
- **Focusing on subscription-based business models**, leading to **higher recurring revenue streams.**

His investment thesis **prioritized long-term growth over short-term exits**, setting him apart from traditional LBO firms.

Legacy:
Bravo's approach positioned **Thoma Bravo as a global leader in technology investing**, competing with firms like Silver Lake and Vista Equity Partners. His **software-focused investment strategy** reshaped the industry and helped define the **modern playbook for tech private equity.**

Why These Leaders Matter in PE Leadership

Each of these **private equity visionaries** reshaped the industry in their own way:

- **Henry Kravis & George Roberts (KKR):** Masterminds of the leveraged buyout.

- **Robert Smith (Vista Equity Partners):** Innovator of tech-driven private equity.

- **Orlando Bravo (Thoma Bravo):** The leader in software consolidation strategies.

Their leadership styles—whether in financial engineering, operational value creation, or tech investing—serve as **critical case studies for modern PE professionals.**

PE Leadership Trivia: Did You Know?

40 Leaders and 40 Trivia

Name	Trivia
Henry Kravis & George Roberts (KKR)	Pioneered the leveraged buyout (LBO) industry, famously acquiring RJR Nabisco for $31.1 billion in 1988, inspiring the book *Barbarians at the Gate*.
David Rubenstein (Carlyle Group)	Before co-founding Carlyle, Rubenstein was a domestic policy advisor to President Jimmy Carter.
Stephen Schwarzman (Blackstone)	Turned a $400,000 investment into Blackstone, now the largest alternative asset manager with over $1 trillion in AUM.
William Conway, Daniel D'Aniello & David Rubenstein (Carlyle Group)	Named the firm after the Carlyle Hotel in New York, reflecting their vision of exclusivity and influence.
Leon Black (Apollo Global Management)	Mastered distressed asset investing, reshaping how PE firms acquire undervalued businesses.
Robert Smith (Vista Equity Partners)	The first Black billionaire in PE, known for paying off the student debt of Morehouse College's graduating class in 2019.
Tony Ressler (Ares Management)	Helped build Apollo Global before co-founding Ares, now one of the largest credit-focused PE firms.
Thomas H. Lee (THL Partners)	Acquired Snapple for $135 million in 1992, selling it two years later for $1.7 billion.

Steve Pagliuca (Bain Capital)	A Bain executive and co-owner of the Boston Celtics, blending sports and finance leadership.
Mitt Romney (Bain Capital)	Led Bain Capital's expansion and later transitioned into politics, serving as a U.S. senator and presidential candidate.
Michael Bloomberg (Bloomberg LP)	Used his PE-style investment mindset to build a media empire after receiving a $10M severance payout from Salomon Brothers.
Jose Feliciano & Behdad Eghbali (Clearlake Capital)	Co-owners of Chelsea FC, integrating PE-style operational strategies into sports management.
Orlando Bravo (Thoma Bravo)	Considered the **"Godfather of Software Private Equity"**, pioneering tech-focused buyouts.
Joe Bae & Scott Nuttall (KKR Co-CEOs)	Took over KKR after Kravis and Roberts stepped down, marking a generational leadership shift.
John Connaughton & Jonathan Lavine (Bain Capital Co-Managing Partners)	Expanded Bain Capital into credit, real estate, and tech investing.
Marc Rowan (Apollo Global CEO)	Transformed Apollo's focus from LBOs to credit and insurance-driven investments.
Jon Gray (Blackstone President & COO)	Made Blackstone the world's largest real estate investor before becoming its President.
Jonathan Nelson (Providence Equity Partners)	One of the first PE investors to focus exclusively on media and telecom industries.
Josh Harris (Apollo & 76ers Owner)	A co-founder of Apollo who later became a major sports investor, owning the **Philadelphia 76ers & Washington Commanders.**

Bruce Flatt (Brookfield Asset Management)	Built Brookfield into one of the largest alternative investment firms, with assets spanning real estate, infrastructure, and renewables.
David Bonderman (TPG Capital)	Early investor in Uber, Airbnb, and Ducati, pioneering tech and hospitality PE deals.
Michael Kim (MBK Partners)	The most influential Asian PE investor, running **MBK Partners, Asia's largest independent PE firm.**
Chris Hohn (TCI Fund Management)	A top **activist investor**, forcing leadership changes in companies like Alphabet (Google's parent).
Joe Baratta (Global Head of PE, Blackstone)	Leads some of Blackstone's biggest deals, particularly in technology and real estate.
Holly Kim (Former KKR, Now at CVC Capital)	One of the most senior female executives in global private equity.
Jean Salata (BPEA EQT, Formerly Baring Private Equity Asia)	Led one of **Asia's largest PE firms**, later acquired by EQT.
David Solomon (Goldman Sachs, PE & CEO)	Led Goldman's expansion into private equity while also working as a part-time DJ.
Mary Meeker (Bond Capital, Former Kleiner Perkins)	One of the **most successful female investors** focusing on internet and software companies.
Tom Barrack (Colony Capital)	Made a fortune investing in distressed **real estate and hospitality assets**, including major hotel chains.
David Siegel & John Overdeck (Two Sigma, PE & Hedge Fund)	Applied **data science and AI to private equity**, blending quant finance with PE deal-making.
Glenn Youngkin (Former Carlyle CEO, Now Governor of Virginia)	Transitioned from **leading one of the biggest PE firms to politics.**

Paul Singer (Elliott Management, Activist PE)	Known for **aggressive activist investing**, forcing major corporate leadership changes at AT&T, Twitter, and eBay.
Sanjay Patel (Head of PE, Apollo Global Management)	Expanded Apollo's **credit and insurance business**, making it a leading non-traditional PE firm.
Stephen Pagliuca (Bain Capital & Celtics Co-Owner)	Blends finance with sports ownership, applying **PE principles to managing the Boston Celtics.**
Kim Kardashian (SKKY Partners)	Founded **SKKY Partners**, one of the first celebrity-led PE firms, focusing on consumer and media investments.
Josh Lerner (Harvard Business School, PE Researcher)	One of the **most influential PE academics**, shaping how the industry understands leadership and value creation.
Adebayo Ogunlesi (Global Infrastructure Partners - GIP)	Runs one of the largest infrastructure-focused PE firms, **owning major airports worldwide.**
Brett Hickey (Star Mountain Capital)	A major investor in the **lower-middle market, focusing on overlooked private equity opportunities.**
Joseph Landy (Warburg Pincus, Former Co-CEO)	Helped Warburg Pincus become one of the leading **growth-focused PE firms.**

Afterword

Leadership in Private Equity: The Path Forward

As we reach the conclusion of this book, I want to extend my deepest appreciation to you—the reader. Whether you are a private equity professional, an aspiring leader, or someone looking to refine your leadership skills in high-stakes environments, your commitment to learning and growth is what defines true leadership.

Throughout this book, we have explored the complexities of leadership within Private Equity—how it differs from traditional corporate leadership, how it requires both strategic thinking and hands-on execution, and how it is evolving with the integration of new technologies. We have discussed frameworks, challenges, and opportunities, but most importantly, we have reinforced the idea that leadership is not about titles or authority—it is about **execution, resilience, and the ability to create value where others see obstacles.**

The best leaders are **lifelong learners**, and I hope this book has provided you with insights, strategies, and tools that you can apply in your own leadership journey. PE is a demanding field, but it is also one that rewards those who **adapt, innovate, and lead with conviction.**

"Leadership is an ongoing journey of learning, adaptation, and service. May this book serve as a stepping stone on your path to leadership mastery."

A Personal Note of Gratitude

Writing this book has been both a challenge and a privilege. I wrote it not just to share knowledge, but to **contribute to the next generation of leaders in private equity**—those who will make the difficult decisions, guide companies through transformation, and leave a lasting impact on the industry.

Thank you for investing your time in this book. Thank you for your curiosity, your ambition, and your willingness to refine your leadership skills. Whether you are leading a deal team, running a portfolio company, or aspiring to do so in the future, I hope the principles shared in these pages help you navigate your journey with confidence and clarity.

Leadership is never about reaching a final destination—it is a continuous process of learning, adapting, and refining. If this book has given you even one new idea, one fresh perspective, or one practical takeaway that strengthens your leadership, then it has fulfilled its purpose.

I look forward to hearing how these insights resonate with you. Until then, keep leading, keep learning, and most importantly—keep creating value.

With appreciation,

Mohamad Chahine

About the Author

Mohamad Chahine: Leadership in Private Equity

Mohamad Chahine is a seasoned **Private Equity (PE) and Venture Capital (VC) leader** with over **25 years of experience** across **four continents and more than 20 countries.** He has **managed portfolios exceeding $10 billion in enterprise value** and has held key leadership roles throughout the **PE lifecycle,** including **Deal Team Member, Operating Partner, Managing Director, Interim, and Fractional CEO.** His expertise spans **buyouts, fund management, value creation, and business transformation.**

His leadership philosophy centers on **driving performance, navigating uncertainty, and building high-impact teams.** With experience leading **turnarounds, executing growth strategies, and managing complex transactions,** he brings a results-driven, hands-on approach to leadership.

Starting his career as an **Oil & Gas Field Engineer at Schlumberger,** he later transitioned into **brand management, strategy consulting, and investment leadership at Investcorp.** This diverse background provides him with a **broad, cross-industry perspective on leadership and investment strategy.**

Expanding Leadership Insights Through Writing

Initially a hobbyist writer, Mohamad has increasingly dedicated time to developing books that serve as **practical resources for professionals navigating leadership, investment, and business transformation.** His work focuses on **Private Equity leadership, value creation strategies, and the evolving role of technology in investment decisions.**

Selected Books by Mohamad Chahine

The Private Equity Essential Primer & Value Creation Toolkit Series

- *Perfecting Leadership in Private Equity*
- *The Operating Partner Playbook*
- *Digital Private Equity*

Future-Proof Leadership Series

- *Extreme CEOing*
- *Unlock Your Potential*
- *The AI Fortune Teller*

Business Culture & Corporate Strategy

- *Cubicles, Coffee, and Corporate Candy*

Mohamad is based in **Mississauga, Ontario,** where he balances his professional work with interests in **archery, DIY electronics, and leadership development.** His guiding philosophy reflects his commitment to **continuous growth and meaningful impact:**

"Aspire to be a better version of myself every day—and help others do the same."

Copyright © 2024 by Mohamad Chahine. All rights reserved. No part of this book may be reproduced, stored, or transmitted in any form or by any means without prior written permission of the author, except in the case of brief quotations embodied in critical reviews and certain other non-commercial uses permitted by copyright law. For permission requests, contact the author.

www.ingramcontent.com/pod-product-compliance
Lightning Source LLC
Chambersburg PA
CBHW070611170426
43200CB00012B/2658